CYBERSPACE OPERATIONS

Air Force Doctrine Document 3-12
15 July 2010

Incorporating Change 1, 30 November 2011

BY ORDER OF THE
SECRETARY OF THE AIR FORCE

AIR FORCE DOCTRINE DOCUMENT 3-12
15 JULY 2010
INCORPORATING CHANGE 1, 30 NOVEMBER 2011 |

SUMMARY OF CHANGES

This interim change reflects updates in national guidance, command relationships, and force presentation. The more significant changes are found in Chapter Two. Updates reflect USSTRATCOM delegation of OPCON to USCYBERCOM (page 20), full operational status of the 624th Operations Center (page 24), normalization of AF cyberspace liaison deployments to theater staffs (page 26), and establishment of the terms "AFCYBER" identifying the 24th Air Force as the Service element to USSTRATCOM (page 21) and "AF cyber tasking order" identifying the CTO as a standard tasking product analogous to an air tasking order (page 30). Lastly, this interim change reflects a more current listing of policy and doctrine in Appendix B and in the References section, and it updates terms and definitions in the Glossary.

OPR: LeMay Center/DDS
Certified by: LeMay Center/DD (Col Todd C. Westhauser)
Pages: 60
Accessibility: Publications are available on the e-publishing website at www.e-publishing.af.mil for downloading
Releasability: There are no releasability restrictions on this publication
Approved by: Thomas K. Andersen, Major General, USAF
Commander, Curtis E. LeMay Center for Doctrine Development and Education

FOREWORD

Today, we live in a globally-networked society that is increasingly dependent upon cyberspace access and security. Our ability to gain and maintain superiority in cyberspace has become essential to our ability to deliver global reach, power, and vigilance. As an integral member of the joint warfighting team, the Air Force is committed to growing, sustaining, and presenting highly skilled and well-equipped forces to joint force commanders who can deliver decisive effects in, from, and through cyberspace, while assuring our mission against an asymmetric cyber threat.

Freedom of action in the cyberspace domain enables our command, control, communication, computers, intelligence, surveillance, and reconnaissance capabilities. Our modern defenses, industrial base, and global commerce, as well as that of our nation's enemies, depend on free use of land, sea, air, space, and cyberspace. Leverage in cyberspace affords influence and control across all other domains. This leverage increases our forces' access, speed, reach, stealth, and precision.

Controlling the portions of cyberspace integral to our mission is a fundamental prerequisite to effective operations across the range of military operations. While we appreciate the power that cyber-enabled capabilities add, we also maintain a healthy respect for the asymmetric power that cyberspace affords our adversaries. We must maintain a constant commitment to educate, train, and equip our Airman to prevail in the contested domain of cyberspace.

In the past decade, we have participated in a revolution in military affairs afforded by cyberspace technologies. Technological advances have provided the means to generate decisive and magnified effects in domains that traditionally could only be achieved via kinetic means. We must continually adapt our operating concepts to leverage emerging cyberspace capabilities to ensure the Air Force maintains the decisive advantage over our adversaries.

Since Airmen use cyberspace capabilities, it is important that Airmen understand cyberspace operations. A cyberspace risk created by one Airman can pose a potential risk for the entire force. Airmen must defend cyberspace capabilities against threats in order to protect mission-critical information and war fighting capabilities. Airmen must make a fundamental commitment to growing our individual and collective knowledge, skills, and abilities throughout the cyberspace domain.

THOMAS K. ANDERSEN
Major General, USAF
Commander, LeMay Center
for Doctrine Development
and Education

TABLE OF CONTENTS

PREFACE

Much has changed in the overall operational environment in the past few years. The character of contemporary conflict has driven a significant shift in the US approach to warfighting. The large-scale, complex, force-on-force scenarios that drove much of Cold War planning, and were executed in Operation DESERT STORM and the opening stage of Operation IRAQI FREEDOM are now viewed almost as the exception, replaced by the careful, precise, and relatively measured pace of irregular warfare against nontraditional enemies. Moreover, it appears that US engagement in such conflicts will be ongoing for the next decade or longer.

The causes of conflict may vary from rational political calculation to uncontrolled actions. Adversary capabilities may range from long-range, precision-guided attacks to explosive vests worn by suicide bombers. The threat of mass destruction from chemical, biological, radiological, and nuclear weapons will likely expand from stable nation-states to less stable states and even non-state networks.[1]

These changes have significant, long-term implications for the planning and conduct of US operations:

⊙ The need for current, precise, and detailed analysis requires a continuing expansion in the scale of information collection and processing; networks are as important as a single bullet or bomb. Sensors, shooters, and fusion centers are routinely interconnected worldwide to achieve a unified battle rhythm.

⊙ Threats against the US homeland will increase. The United States can expect future opponents to launch both terrorist and unconventional attacks on the territory of the United States.[2] Civil, military, and industrial cyber networks have already seen an upswing in probes, intrusions, exploitations, and attacks.

The proliferation of commercially available technology will allow adversaries to develop niche capabilities that will threaten, in varying degrees, the successful conduct of operations in areas where US forces were previously unchallenged. Space and cyber networks are increasingly vulnerable to a wide array of new threats. Adversary anti-access capabilities will continue to improve, challenging US ability to project power and influence.[3] Countering these capabilities is vital to assure freedom of action in, through, and from air, space, and cyberspace.

Air Force Doctrine Document (AFDD) 3-12, *Cyberspace Operations*, is the Air Force's foundational doctrine publication for Air Force operations in, through, and from

---

[1] United States Joint Forces Command Publication, "*Joint Operational Environment 2008 – Changes and Implications for the Future Joint Force*," November 25, 2008, (JOE); and HQ USAF/A8X draft "*Future Operating Environment*" (FOE), 2008.

[2] HQ USAF/A8X draft "*Future Operating Environment*" (FOE), 2008, p. 7.

[3] FOE, p. 9.

the cyberspace domain. AFDD 3-12 represents known sanctioned ideas and practices in the three chapters described below. This document means to provide insight for Airmen to follow. This document speaks to Air Force support of maintaining Cyberspace Superiority, a common military function.

Chapter 1, Cyberspace Fundamentals. Chapter 1 establishes the fundamental nature and context of Air Force cyberspace operations in this newly defined operational environment. This chapter defines fundamental terms and concepts for cyberspace operations. Discussions in this chapter include the strategic environment, general strategic policy, missions, military challenges, the Airman's perspective, relationship to other doctrine, principles of war, tenets of airpower, and cross-domain integration.

Chapter 2, Command and Organization. Chapter 2 describes the command, control, and organization of cyberspace forces. It depicts operational-level policy, command relationships, and commander roles and responsibilities. It discusses how global and theater cyberspace operations will be conducted through integrated command, control, and organization of military capabilities to achieve JFC objectives.

Chapter 3, Design, Planning, Execution, and Assessment. Chapter 3 describes how Air Force cyberspace operations are designed, planned, executed, and assessed. Also described are legal concerns, logistics, and operational considerations across the range of military operations.

Appendix A, Ten Things Every Airman Must Know. This is a list of ten things that every Airman ought to know, with respect to cyberspace operations.

Appendix B, Policy and Doctrine Related to Cyberspace Operations. This matrix includes recent and relevant National, Department of Defense-level, joint, and Air Force documents, publications, and doctrine which are related to cyberspace operations.

CHAPTER ONE

CYBERSPACE FUNDAMENTALS

We have moved past the civilities in the cyberspace domain. US forces and those of our adversaries now rely heavily on their computer networks for command and control, for intelligence, for planning, for communications, and for conducting operations. But these architectures are vulnerable. In fact for more than 15 years, the US government and DOD networks have come under increasing pressure to attacks and probes from adversaries, as diverse as nation-states, to disgruntled individuals or bored teenage hackers. And while we have detected illicit activities on our networks for more than 15 years and employed dual resources to offer a comprehensive multi-disciplinary approach to protecting our networks, we need to do more.

—General Kevin Chilton, USAF
Commander, US Strategic Command, in
"Cyberspace Leadership: Towards
New Culture, Conduct, and
Capabilities,"
***Air & Space Power Journal*, Fall 2009**

DEFINITIONS

Cyberspace.   Cyberspace is "a global domain within the information environment consisting of the interdependent network of information technology infrastructures, including the Internet, telecommunications networks, computer systems, and embedded processors and controllers."[4]

Cyberspace operations. "The employment of cyberspace capabilities where the primary purpose is to achieve military objectives or effects in or through cyberspace."[5]

---

[4] Joint Publication (JP) 1-02, *Department of Defense Dictionary of Military and Associated Terms*
[5] JP 3-0

Cyberspace superiority. The operational advantage in, through, and from cyberspace to conduct operations at a given time and in a given domain without prohibitive interference.[6]

Cyberspace superiority may be localized in time and space, or it may be broad and enduring. The concept of cyberspace superiority hinges on the idea of preventing prohibitive interference to joint forces from opposing forces, which would prevent joint forces from creating their desired effects. "Supremacy" prevents effective interference, which does not mean that no interference exists, but that any attempted interference can be countered or should be so negligible as to have little or no effect on operations. While "supremacy" is most desirable, it may not be operationally feasible. Cyberspace superiority, even local or mission-specific cyberspace superiority, may provide sufficient freedom of action to create desired effects. Therefore, commanders should determine the minimum level of control required to accomplish their mission and assign the appropriate level of effort.

UNDERSTANDING CYBERSPACE

Cyberspace is a domain. Cyberspace operations are not synonymous with information operations (IO). IO is a set of operations that can be performed in cyberspace and other domains. Operations in cyberspace can directly support IO and non-cyber based IO can affect cyberspace operations.

Cyberspace is a man-made domain, and is therefore unlike the natural domains of air, land, maritime, and space. It requires continued attention from humans to persist and encompass the features of specificity, global scope, and emphasis on the electromagnetic spectrum. Cyberspace nodes physically reside in all domains. Activities in cyberspace can enable freedom of action for activities in the other domains, and activities in the other domains can create effects in and through cyberspace.

Even though networks in cyberspace are interdependent, parts of these networks are isolated. Isolation in cyberspace exists via protocols, firewalls, encryption, and physical separation from other networks. For instance, classified networks such as the US Armed Forces Secure Internet Protocol Router network (SIPRnet) are not hardwired to the Internet at all times, but connect to it via secure portals. Additionally, the construction of some hard-wired networks isolates them from most forms of radio frequency (RF) interference. These factors enable these networks to be isolated within cyberspace, yet still allow controlled connectivity to global networks.

Cyberspace segments are connected and supported by physical infrastructure, electronic systems, and portions of the electromagnetic spectrum (EMS).[7] As new

---

[6] Approved Air Force Space Command (AFSPC) definition of cyberspace superiority, derived from multiple AFSPC and LeMay Center cyberspace operations working groups, 2009-2010.
[7] Definition of electromagnetic spectrum (EMS): "The range of frequencies of electromagnetic radiation from zero to infinity. It is divided into 26 alphabetically designated bands." (JP 3-13.1)

systems and infrastructures are developed, they may use increasing portions of the EMS, have higher data processing capacity and speed, and leverage greater bandwidth. Systems may also be designed to change frequencies (the places where they operate within the EMS) as they manipulate data. Thus, physical maneuver space exists in cyberspace.[8]

Logical maneuverability in cyberspace is often a function of the security protocols used by host systems. Systems seeking connectivity with a secure host will have more difficulty gaining access than systems seeking connectivity with unsecured hosts. Additionally, defense against entry by undesired systems resides in the code or logic of the host system. Once a connection between systems is established, a potential intruder must exploit a fault in logic to enter the system. Code writing can thus be a form of logical maneuver in cyberspace. The potential intruder writes malicious code to gain maneuverability against targeted systems. As a defender becomes aware of unwanted presence within the system, the defender will alter the system's code to deny entry. The intruder, wishing to remain "on target," adapts the malicious code accordingly. This process is the equivalent of forces maneuvering to gain positions of advantage in the traditional air, land, space, and maritime domains. Both logical and physical maneuver space is required — one is often useless without the other.

THE OPERATIONAL ENVIRONMENT

The cyberspace domain is now a primary conduit for transactions vital to every facet of modern life. Our society and military are increasingly dependent on cyberspace. Cyberspace is a source of both strength and vulnerability for modern society. While cyberspace operations enable a modern society, they also create critical vulnerabilities for our adversaries to attack or exploit. Manufacturing controls, public utilities distribution, banking, communications, and the distribution of information for national security have shifted to networked systems. While this 30-year evolution has significantly benefited society, it has also created serious vulnerabilities. Increased wireless dependence and expanded interconnectivity has exposed previously isolated critical infrastructures vital to national security, public health, and economic well-being. Adversaries may attempt to deny, degrade, manipulate, disrupt, or destroy critical infrastructures through cyberspace attack, thus affecting warfighting systems and the nation as a whole. Recent incursions into Department of Defense (DOD) and Air Force networks underscore today's cyberspace challenge.

Adversaries in cyberspace are exploiting low-entry costs, widely available resources, and minimal required technological investment to inflict serious harm, resulting in an increasingly complex and distributed environment. The expanded availability of commercial off-the-shelf (COTS) technology provides adversaries with increasingly flexible and affordable technology to adapt to military purposes. Low barriers to entry significantly decrease the traditional capability gap between the US and

---

[8] For additional information on the "Physical, Syntactic, and Semantic layers of Cyberspace" see Chapter 10 of "*Conquest in Cyberspace,*" Libicki, Martin C., RAND Corporation, Cambridge University Press, 2007.

our adversaries. Adversaries are fielding sophisticated cyberspace systems and experimenting with advanced warfighting concepts.

Cyberspace Infrastructure Relationships[9]

The Air Force depends upon the US' critical infrastructure and key resources for many of its activities, including force deployment, training, transportation, and normal operations. Physical protection of these is no longer sufficient as most critical infrastructure is under the control of networked and interdependent supervisory control and data acquisition (SCADA) or distributed control systems (DCS).

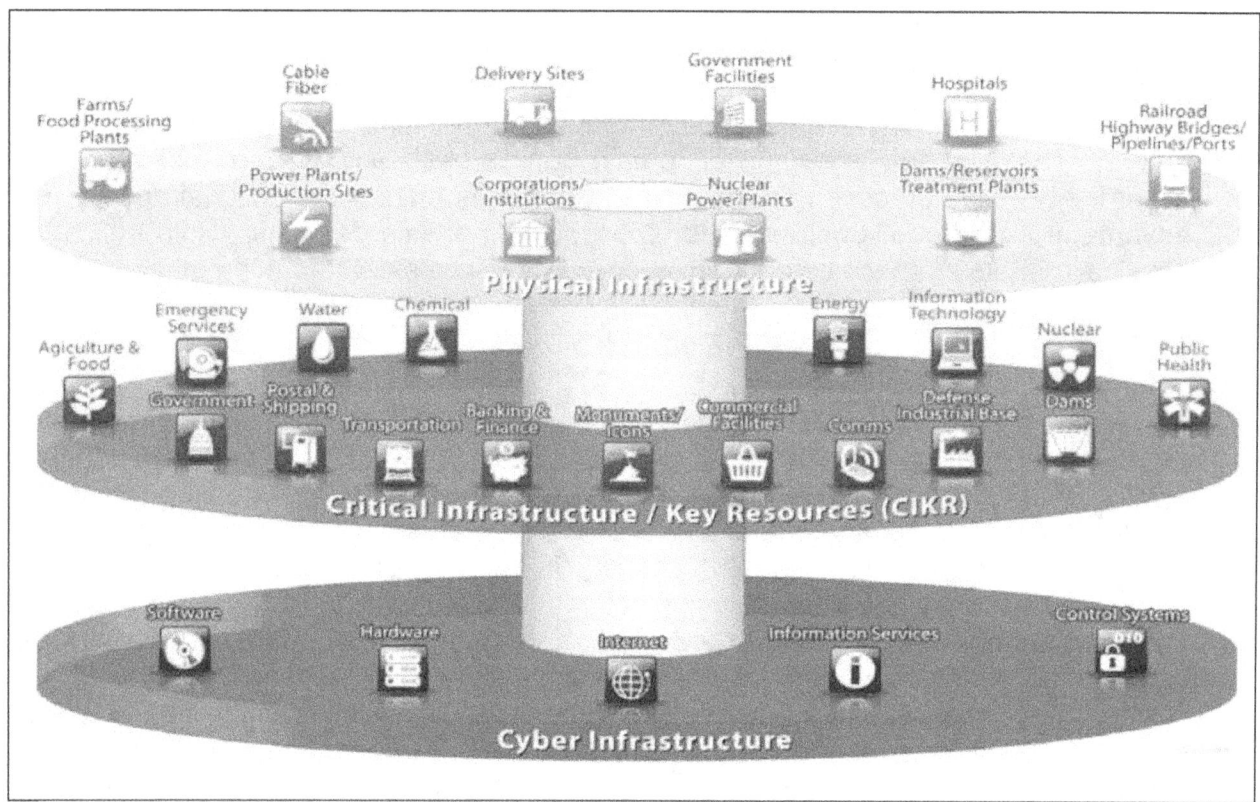

Figure 1.1. Cyber Infrastructure

Since private industry is the primary catalyst for technological advancements, the military may become increasingly reliant on COTS technology. This reliance may present three primary vulnerabilities:

---

[9] Adapted from DHS: "Securing the Nation's Critical Cyber Infrastructure."

○ Foreign ownership, control, and influence of vendors. Many of the COTS technologies (hardware and software) the Air Force purchases are developed, manufactured, or have components manufactured by foreign countries. These manufacturers, vendors, service providers, and developers can be influenced by adversaries to provide altered products that have built-in vulnerabilities, such as modified chips.

○ Supply chain. The global supply chain has vulnerabilities that can potentially lead to the interception and alteration of products. These vulnerabilities are present throughout the product life cycle, from the inception of the design concept, to product delivery, and to product updates and support.

○ COTS and government off-the-shelf (GOTS) balance. The vast majority of the Air Force's cyberspace operations components and capabilities are from COTS and to a much smaller degree, GOTS technologies.

US NATIONAL CYBERSPACE POLICY

We are in the midst of a dramatic change in the relationship between technology and the nature of warfare.

—David J. Lonsdale
The Nature of War in the Information Age: Clausewitzian Future

There are many policy documents pertaining to cyberspace operations policy. The documents most relevant to Air Force cyberspace operations are in Appendix B, *Policy and Doctrine Related to Cyberspace Operations*.

The *Comprehensive National Cybersecurity Initiative* (CNCI) consists of a number of mutually reinforcing initiatives with the following major goals designed to help secure the United States in cyberspace:

○ To establish a front line of defense against today's immediate threats by creating or enhancing shared situational awareness of network vulnerabilities, threats, and events within the Federal Government—and ultimately with state, local, and tribal governments and private sector partners—and the ability to act quickly to reduce our current vulnerabilities and prevent intrusions.

○ To defend against the full spectrum of threats by enhancing US counterintelligence capabilities and increasing the security of the supply chain for key information technologies.

✪   To strengthen the future cybersecurity environment by expanding cyber education, coordinating and redirecting research and development efforts across the Federal Government, and working to define and develop strategies to deter hostile or malicious activity in cyberspace.

The following information is extracted from the CNCI[10]:

"[The President] has identified cybersecurity as one of the most serious economic and national security challenges we face as a nation, but one that we as a government or as a country are not adequately prepared to counter. Shortly after taking office, the President therefore ordered a thorough review of federal efforts to defend the US information and communications infrastructure and the development of a comprehensive approach to securing America's digital infrastructure. In May 2009, the President accepted the recommendations of the resulting Cyberspace Policy Review, including the selection of an Executive Branch Cybersecurity Coordinator who will have regular access to the President. The Executive Branch was also directed to work closely with all key players in US cybersecurity, including state and local governments and the private sector, to ensure an organized and unified response to future cyber incidents; strengthen public/private partnerships to find technology solutions that ensure US security and prosperity; invest in the cutting-edge research and development necessary for the innovation and discovery to meet the digital challenges of our time; and begin a campaign to promote cybersecurity awareness and digital literacy from our boardrooms to our classrooms and begin to build the digital workforce of the 21st century. Finally, the President directed that these activities be conducted in a way that is consistent with ensuring the privacy rights and civil liberties guaranteed in the Constitution and cherished by all Americans."

The *National Strategy to Secure Cyberspace* is the comprehensive strategy for the US to secure cyberspace. It spells out three strategic priorities:

✪   Prevent cyber attacks against America's critical infrastructure

✪   Reduce national vulnerability to cyber attacks

✪   Minimize damage and recovery time from cyber attacks

The *National Strategy to Secure Cyberspace* seeks to empower US citizens to secure the portions of cyberspace that they own, operate, control, or with which they interact. This document outlines the framework for organizing and prioritizing US Government efforts in cyberspace. This strategy guides federal government departments and agencies that secure cyberspace. It identifies the steps every individual can take to improve our collective cyberspace security.

---

[10] The Comprehensive National Cybersecurity Initiative (CNCI), The White House, DECLASSIFIED 2010.

The *National Military Strategy for Cyberspace Operations* (NMS-CO) is the comprehensive strategy for US Armed Forces to ensure US superiority in cyberspace. There are four strategic priorities of the NMS-CO:

✪ Gain and maintain initiative to operate within adversary decision cycles

✪ Integrate cyberspace capabilities across the range of military operations (ROMO)

✪ Build capacity for cyberspace operations

✪ Manage risk for operations in cyberspace

The NMS-CO describes the cyberspace domain, articulates cyberspace threats and vulnerabilities, and provides a strategic framework for action. The NMS-CO is the US Armed Forces' comprehensive strategic approach for using cyberspace operations to assure US military strategic superiority in the domain. The integration of offensive and defensive cyberspace operations, coupled with the skill and knowledge of our people, is fundamental to this approach.

CHALLENGES OF CYBERSPACE OPERATIONS

Cyberspace operations offer unique military challenges. The paragraphs below address some of the known challenges: mission assurance, a compressed decision cycle, anonymity and the attribution challenge, and various threats inherent to cyberspace itself.

There is a requirement to balance defensive cyberspace actions within cyberspace with their impact on ongoing air, space, and cyberspace operations. The lack of situational awareness among domains can cause serious disconnects in one, significantly hindering operations in others.[11]

Mission Assurance

Mission assurance consists of measures required to accomplish essential objectives of missions in a contested environment.[12] Mission assurance entails prioritizing mission essential functions (MEFs), mapping mission dependence on cyberspace, identifying vulnerabilities, and mitigating risk of known vulnerabilities.

Mission assurance ensures the availability of a secured network to support military operations by assuring and defending the portion of the network directly supporting the operation. Cyberspace mission assurance begins by mapping the operation to the supporting architecture. Then, deliberate actions are taken to assure the availability of that portion of the network. These may include adding backups to

---

[11] Office of Air Force Lessons Learned, *Enduring Airpower Lessons from OEF/OIF, Cyberspace Freedom of Action,* 20-25 April 2009, HQ USAF A9.

[12] United States Scientific Advisory Board, *Report on Defending and Operating in a Contested Cyber Domain,* SAB-TR-08-01, August 2008, p. 11.

single points of failure in the network or delaying certain maintenance actions to ensure the network will meet mission requirements. Second, the proactive actions are taken to ensure the network is secure and defended. These actions may include focusing the attention of network defense assets on the slice of the network supporting the operations and conducting operations to ensure no threats are resident on the network.

A "contested cyber environment" involves circumstances in which one or more adversaries attempt to change the outcome of a mission by denying, degrading, disrupting, or destroying our cyber capabilities, or by altering the usage, product, or our confidence in those capabilities.[13]

Warfighters should realize risks and vulnerabilities are often created by the interdependencies inherent in the networking and integration of systems through cyberspace. Integration of cyberspace operations involves actions taken to enable decision superiority through command and control (C2), innovation, integration, and standardization of systems across air, space, and cyberspace domains. Integration means are tested via operational experiments like the Joint Expeditionary Force Experiment. Identifying vulnerabilities is difficult within a contested cyber environment. Our systems are open to assault and are difficult to defend. Some known examples of vulnerabilities in cyberspace operations are listed in the NMS-CO.

Assuring missions via cyberspace operations involves risk. Since the nature of cyberspace is interconnectivity, all cyberspace operations have inherent risk requiring constant attention and mitigation. Cyberspace is a domain with its own set of risks. In this domain, a risk assumed by one is potentially assumed by all. Mitigation of risk can result in a decreased risk level considered acceptable to continue conducting operations.[14] Examples of this kind of approach toward handling risk can be seen in many aspects. The implementation of firewalls, training, education, and intrusion detection and prevention systems represent types of risk mitigation.

Just as in the air domain, we do not defend the entire cyberspace domain; we defend what is relevant to our operations. In cyberspace, this means protecting pathways and components, since action against critical systems could seriously degrade our ability to fight and win. Whether used offensively or defensively, however, conducting particular cyberspace operations may require access to only a very small "slice" of the domain. This does not mean "localized" in the sense of a limited geographical area (although that too may sometimes be required), but perhaps just a string of internet protocol (IP) addresses, which may span the globe but represent only a miniscule portion of data flow bandwidth. Similarly, it may involve the ability to hack through one particular firewall that may physically reside upon several servers, but which is never engaged physically only through virtual means. Finally, many operations may span only seconds from inception to conclusion, given the speed at which the Internet operates. Successfully operating in cyberspace may require abandoning common assumptions concerning time and space.

---

[13] Ibid.
[14] The White House, *National Military Strategy for Cyberspace Operations*, 2006.

Freedom of action in cyberspace is a basic requirement for mission assurance. However, having the cyberspace capacity to achieve this freedom of action should not be taken for granted. Just as operating in the air domain requires having the capacity to do so (airborne platforms, runways, etc.), the Air Force should ensure it acquires sufficient capacity (bandwidth, components, etc.) to operate within cyberspace. Since access to cyberspace permeates daily activities, it is easy to overlook this requirement and assume that sufficient capacity will simply exist.

Cyberspace operations seek to ensure freedom of action across all domains for US forces and allies, and deny that same freedom to adversaries. Specifically, cyberspace operations overcome the limitations of distance, time, and physical barriers present in other domains. Exploiting improved technologies makes it possible to enhance the Air Force's global operations by delivering larger information payloads and increasingly sophisticated effects. Cyberspace links operations in other domains thus facilitating interdependent defensive, exploitative, and offensive operations to achieve situational advantage.

Potential adversaries wish to undermine mission assurance actions via cyberspace operations. The Air Force ensures it can establish and maintain cyberspace superiority and fight through cyberspace attacks at any time regardless if the US requires the use of military forces. Our adversaries have also demonstrated that they can create civil instability through cyber attacks. The Air Force maintains a capability to provide defense support to civil authorities in cyberspace when called upon by national leadership. Potential adversaries have declared and demonstrated their intent; Russia's relatively crude ground offensive into Georgia in 2008 was preceded by a widespread and well-coordinated cyberspace attack. The massive cyberspace attack and ensuing effects suffered by Estonia in 2007 illustrate how quickly malicious hackers affect even a technologically sophisticated government.

One last point to highlight concerning mission assurance is homeland infrastructure protection from threats or natural disaster. The Air Force should prepare to respond rapidly to mitigate effects of such threats or events and reconstitute lost critical infrastructure capabilities while also providing support to civil authorities as directed by competent authority. The Air Force should establish policies and guidance to ensure the execution of mission essential functions for critical infrastructure protection, in the event that an emergency threatens or incapacitates operations.

Compressed Decision Cycle of Cyberspace Operations

The fact that operations can take place nearly instantaneously requires the formulation of appropriate responses to potential cyberspace attacks within legal and policy constraints. The compressed decision cycle may require predetermined rules for intelligence, surveillance, and reconnaissance (ISR) actions.

Anonymity and the Inherent Attribution Challenge

Perhaps the most challenging aspect of attribution of actions in cyberspace is connecting a cyberspace actor or action to an actual, real-world agent (be it individual or state actor) with sufficient confidence and verifiability to inform decision- and policy-makers. Often this involves significant analysis and collaboration with other, non-cyberspace agencies or organizations. While cyberspace attribution (e.g., indentifying a particular IP address) may be enough for some actions, such as establishing access lists (e.g., "white" or "black" lists of allowed or blocked IP addresses), attribution equating to positive identification of the IP address holder may be required for others, such as offensive actions targeting identified IP addresses.

The nature of cyberspace, government policies, and international laws and treaties make it very difficult to determine the origin of a cyberspace attack. The ability to hide the source of an attack makes it difficult to connect an attack with an attacker within the cyberspace domain. The design of the Internet lends itself to anonymity.

Anonymity is maintained both by the massive volume of information flowing through the networks, and by features that allow users to cloak their identity and activities. Nations can do little to combat the anonymity their adversaries exploit in cyberspace; however, the same features used by terrorists, hackers, and criminals, strengthen state surveillance and law enforcement capability, in modified form. Actions of anonymous or unidentified actors are akin to an arms race. Illicit actors continually amaze those in global law enforcement with the speed at which they stay one step ahead in the technology race. Nevertheless, nations have the advantage of law and the ability to modify the technological environment by regulation.

Anonymity is a feature of the Internet because of the way information moves through it and the way it is governed. The underlying architecture was intended to be robust, distributed, and survivable. The anonymous nature of the Internet is literally written into the structure of the Internet itself and cannot be dislodged without physically destroying many networks. The Internet was also designed where the intelligence was placed at the ends of the network, not in the network itself. Routing tools, software applications, and information requests come from the ends, in contrast to a traditional telephone network in which the switches, routing protocols, etc., are in the network itself. The difference makes it much harder to trace individual bits of information once they are in the network. The Internet's governance structure reflects its design.[15] This makes attribution a challenge.

Threats to Cyberspace Operations

In other domains, the primary threats to national security come from either nation states or transnational actors, such as terrorist organizations. Massive capital resources and personnel are required to build, field, maintain, and operate fighter aircraft, satellites, and ships, but it took only a small and determined organization with simple tools to fly into the World Trade Center buildings on September 11, 2001.

---

[15] Ibid.

Adversaries seek asymmetric advantages and cyberspace provides significant opportunities for obtaining them.

There are a variety of threats to cyberspace operations. The following paragraphs provide a brief description of each category of threat. These threats and others should be considered when conducting cyberspace operations.[16]

Nation State Threat. This threat is potentially the most dangerous because of access to resources, personnel, and time that may not be available to other actors. Other nations may employ cyberspace to attack and conduct espionage against the US. Nation state threats involve traditional adversaries and sometimes, in the case of espionage, even traditional allies. Nation states may conduct operations directly or may outsource third parties to achieve their goals.

Transnational Actor Threat. Transnational actors are formal and informal organizations that are not bound by national borders. These actors use cyberspace to raise funds, communicate with target audiences and each other, recruit, plan operations, destabilize confidence in governments, and conduct direct terrorist action.

Criminal Organization Threat. Criminal organizations may be national or transnational in nature depending on how they are organized. Criminal organizations steal information for their own use or, in turn, sell it to raise capital.

Individual or Small Group Threat. Individuals or small groups of people can illegally disrupt or gain access to a network or computer system—these people are better known as "hackers." The intentions of hackers vary. Some are peaceful and hack into systems to discover vulnerabilities, sometimes sharing the information with the owners and some have malicious intent. Other hackers have political motivations and use cyberspace to spread their message to target audiences. Another type of hacker desires fame or status, and obtains it by breaking into secure systems or creating malware that creates havoc on commercial or government systems. Malware is the short name for "malicious software." Hackers can also be exploited by the other cyberspace threats, such as criminal organizations, in order to execute concealed operations against specific targets while preserving their identity or create plausible deniability.

---

[16] See the *National Military Strategy for Cyberspace Operations,* (2006), for expanded descriptions.

In May 05, an unknown subject obtained unauthorized user level access to the Assignments Management System (AMS). Using this access, the subject was able to view information contained within the AMS, but was unable to alter information or gain access to any other Air Force computer systems. Computer records indicate that the subject gained access to AMS via a senior Air Force official's account. The compromised AMS account was set with privileges which allow the user to review any active duty Air Force members' single unit retrieval format (SURF) data from anywhere in the world with an Internet connection. SURF records contain sensitive data, such as assignment history, security clearance, personal identification information, rank, position, and duty status. The subject gained access to the web based account using the "forgot password" function to answer the challenge questions required to change the account password. The challenge questions asked for biographical information on the senior official, which was readily available on the Internet.

Upon review, it was determined that the senior USAF official's account had been used to view the SURF records of 37,069 Air Force members. Log analysis indicates the intrusion initially originated from forty-one different source IP addresses throughout the duration that the compromised account was used by the subject.

Throughout this duration the subject's activity originated from approximately twelve additional US based Internet Protocol (IP) addresses, which were later determined to be open proxies that the subject used to mask their true place of origin. There were no foreign based IP addresses used after the incident was reported. Court order subpoenas were served on all US-based source IP addresses from which the compromised AMS account was accessed; fifty in total. Information obtained via court order subpoenas identified the last known point of the origin. However, local law enforcement indicated that the information required to further identify the subject was no longer available.

—Air Force Office of Special Investigations Brief, June 2005

Traditional Threat. Traditional threats typically arise from states employing recognized military capabilities and forces in well-understood forms of military conflict. Within cyberspace, these threats may be less understood due to the continuing evolution of technologies and methods. Traditional threats are generally focused against the cyberspace capabilities that enable our air, land, maritime, special operations, and space forces and are focused to deny the US military freedom of action and use of cyberspace.

Irregular Threat. Irregular threats can use cyberspace as an unconventional asymmetric means to counter traditional advantages. These threats could also manifest through an adversary's selective targeting of US cyberspace capabilities and infrastructure. For example, terrorists could use cyberspace to conduct operations against our financial and industrial sectors while simultaneously launching other physical attacks. Terrorists also use cyberspace to communicate anonymously, asynchronously, and without being tied to set physical locations. They attempt to shield themselves from US law enforcement, intelligence, and military operations through use of commercial security products and services readily available in cyberspace. Irregular threats from criminal elements and advocates of radical political agendas seek to use cyberspace for their own ends to challenge government, corporate, or societal interests.

Catastrophic Threat. Catastrophic threats involve the acquisition, possession, and use of weapons of mass destruction (WMD) or methods producing WMD-like effects. While WMD attacks are physical (kinetic) events, they may have profound effects within the cyber domain by degrading or destroying key cyber-based systems vital to infrastructure like SCADA systems. Well-planned attacks on key nodes of the cyberspace infrastructure have the potential to produce network collapse and cascading effects that can severely affect critical infrastructures locally, nationally, or possibly even globally. For example, an electromagnetic pulse could cause widespread damage to segments of the cyberspace domain in which operations must occur.

Disruptive Threat. Disruptive threats are breakthrough technologies that may negate or reduce current US advantages in warfighting domains. Global research, investment, development, and industrial processes provide an environment conducive to the creation of technological advances. The DOD should be prepared for the increased possibility of adversary breakthroughs due to continuing diffusion of cyberspace technologies.

Natural Threat. Natural threats that can damage and disrupt cyberspace include events such as floods, hurricanes, solar flares, lightning, and tornados. These types of events often produce highly destructive effects requiring the DOD to maintain or restore key cyberspace systems. These events also provide adversaries the opportunity to capitalize on infrastructure degradation and diversion of attention and resources.

Accidental Threat. Accidental threats are unpredictable and can take many forms. From a backhoe cutting a fiber optic cable of a key cyberspace node, to inadvertent introduction of viruses, accidental threats unintentionally disrupt the operation of cyberspace. Although post-accident investigations show that the large majority of accidents can be prevented and measures put in place to reduce accidents, accidents should be anticipated.

Insider Threat. The "insider" is an individual currently or at one time authorized to access an organization's information system, data, or network. Such authorization implies a degree of trust in the individual. The insider threat refers to harmful acts that trusted insiders might carry out; for example, something that causes harm to the organization, or an unauthorized act that benefits the individual.

THE AIRMAN'S PERSPECTIVE

Airmen normally think of the application of force from a functional rather than geographical perspective. Airmen do not divide up the battlefield into operating areas as do surface forces; air mindedness entails thinking beyond two dimensions, into the dimensions of the vertical and the dimension of time.[17] Airmen leverage speed, range, flexibility, precision, time, and lethality to create effects from and within the air, space, and cyberspace domains.

Cyberspace operations are intrinsic to the conduct of modern military operations. "Airmen conduct a greater percentage of operations not just over the horizon but globally, expanding operations first through space and now also in cyberspace. Just as air operations grew from its initial use as an adjunct to surface operations, space and cyberspace have likewise grown from their original manifestations as supporting capabilities into warfighting arenas in their own right."[18] Thus, cyberspace operations should be tightly integrated with capabilities of the air and space domains into a cohesive whole, commanded by an Airman who takes a broader view of war, unconstrained by geographic boundaries.

RELATIONSHIP TO OTHER DOCTRINE

Cyberspace operations are compatible with existing Air Force air, space, and IO doctrine. The relevant AFDDs to this document are explained in Appendix B, *Policy and Doctrine Related to Cyberspace Operations*.

Cyberspace operations are integral to all combatant commands, Services, and agency boundaries. As of the date of publication of this AFDD, a new joint publication (JP), JP 3-12 *Cyberspace Operations*, is being developed to provide overarching joint doctrine for planning or operations in cyberspace. Air Force doctrine seeks compatibility and to influence joint doctrine. AFDD 3-12 links cyberspace doctrine to joint operations, including JP 3-13, *Information Operations*. AFDD 3-12 also expands upon concepts found in NATO publications such as Allied Joint Publication (AJP) 3-10, *Information Operations* (see Appendix B).

---

[17] AFDD 1, *Air Force Basic Doctrine, Organization and Command*.
[18] Ibid.

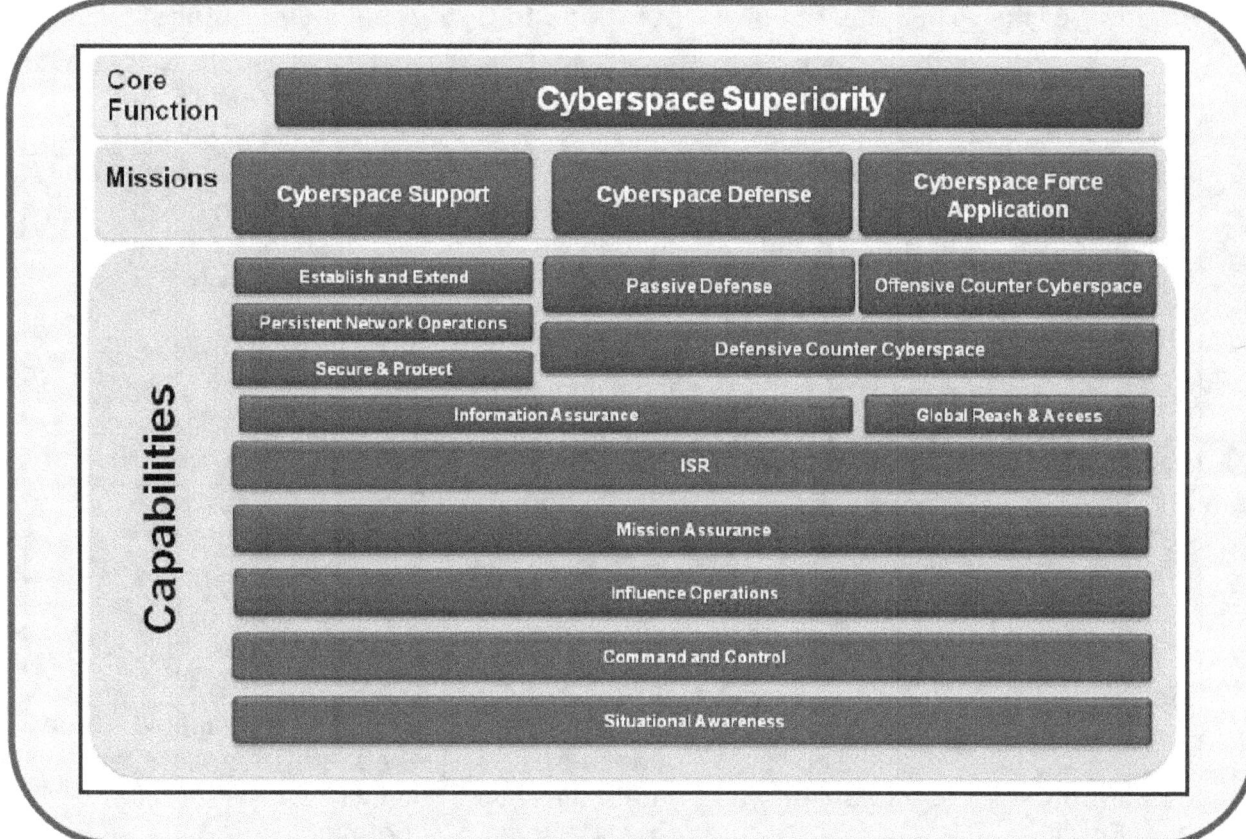

Figure 1.2. Cyberspace Superiority[19]

Cyberspace superiority supports and is supported by all of the other Air Force core functions. It supports our joint and Service doctrine and joint operations concepts by providing cyberspace force application; cyberspace defense; and cyberspace support and associated capabilities that are tailored specifically to cyberspace superiority and are focused to bolster coalition and joint operations. Cyberspace superiority is considered a common military function.

The Air Force approach to cyberspace operations should address, and remain vigilant of, alternative operating principles and procedures. Some cyberspace users have ways and intents of using cyberspace that are similar to our own. Other users (possible adversaries) often operate in ways not constrained by our laws or moral values. Therefore, the US should continue to watch closely for malicious use of cyberspace which can hamper Air Force cyberspace operations.

THE PRINCIPLES OF JOINT OPERATIONS AND CYBERSPACE

Below is a matrix portraying how the principles of joint operations can be expressed and demonstrated through cyberspace operations.[20]

---

[19] Derived from the Cyberspace Superiority Core Function Master Plan.
[20] Per AFDD 1, *Air Force Basic Doctrine*, 17 November 2003.

Relation of the Principles of Joint Operations to Cyberspace Operations[21]

PRINCIPLE	PURPOSE	REMARKS	EXAMPLE CYBERSPACE OPERATION
Objective	Direct every military operation toward a clearly defined, decisive, achievable goal	Military objectives must support overarching political goals	JFC-directed cyberspace attacks shutting down electrical power to key power grids of enemy leadership
Offensive	Disrupt, degrade, deny, deter, seize, retain, and exploit initiative	Most effective, decisive way to achieve objectives	Distributed denial of service attacks on Estonia, 2007, overwhelming Estonian networks
Mass	Concentrate effects at the most advantageous places and times	Must integrate and synchronize with other forces	Suspected Russian actors preemptive attacks on Georgian networks to disrupt coordination of Georgian forces during 2008 invasion
Economy of Force	Allocate minimum essential power to secondary efforts	Less manpower needed to create massive effects across the cyberspace domain	Use of cyberspace attack on key enemy nodes to free "kinetic" assets for other operations
Maneuver	Place the enemy in a position of disadvantage	Keeps enemy off balance	Use of numerous IPs to avoid attribution during a cyber attack.
Unity of Command	Ensure unity of effort under one responsible commander	Attempts to secure unity of effort	Control of Air Force global information grid through the 24 AF
Security	Maintain access without interruption	Reduce friendly vulnerability to hostile acts, influence, and surprise	Protect and enable operability of C2 networks through layered defense, self-healing, and robust reconfigurations
Surprise	Strike at time, place, or manner for which the enemy is unprepared	Can shift advantage well out of proportion to effort expended	Cyberspace attacks that are unannounced on vulnerable or compromised systems

---

[21] Convertino, Sebastian, *Flying and Fighting in Cyberspace,* July 2007, Air University, p. 49.

PRINCIPLE	PURPOSE	REMARKS	EXAMPLE CYBERSPACE OPERATION
Simplicity	Give clear and concise direction to ensure understanding	Minimizes "friction" of war to the maximum extent possible	Equip the force at all levels with user-friendly access to data and network structures
Restraint	Limit collateral damage, prevent unnecessary force	Prevent damaging political and social consequences	Provide stand-alone, non-kinetic options to commanders; creating effects without destroying targets
Perseverance	Ensure commitment necessary to attain strategic end state	War is seldom, if ever, concluded by "the single, sharp blow"	Provide enduring assured operation of systems; create robust cyberspace capability in partner nations
Legitimacy	Ensure actions are legal, moral, and legitimate in eyes of target population and coalition partners	Build trust and cooperation necessary to achieve end state	Use of nonkinetic cyber means to create desired effects against the enemy that under the circumstances are advantageous over kinetic attack

TENETS OF AIRPOWER IN RELATION TO CYBERSPACE OPERATIONS

While the principles of joint operations provide general guidance on the application of military forces, the tenets of airpower provide unique considerations for air and space forces. They reflect the specific lessons of air, space and cyberspace operations over history.

TENET	PURPOSE	REMARKS	EXAMPLE CYBERSPACE OPERATION
Centralized Control, Decentralized Execution	Control by a commander with an Airman's broad perspective; execution by those who best understand the tactical intricacies of a dynamic operation	Enables most effective C2 of capabilities and forces	Geographic combatant commander cyberspace operations concepts of operations which translate into actions taken via regional combined air operations centers (CAOCs) and local Network Operations Centers
Flexibility and Versatility	Exploit mass and maneuver simultaneously; employ at all levels of war	Flexible and versatile cyberspace operations act as a total force multiplier.	Flexibility (simultaneous mass and maneuver) is inherent in the nature of cyberspace itself Versatility also inherent: one small piece of code can create tactical, operational, or strategic effects, depending on the target
Synergistic Effects	Integrate use of forces to create effects that exceed contributions of individual force elements	Ability to freely observe operational environment allowing unprecedented speed and agility	Support integration through robust, persistent and survivable connectivity of C2 and ISR supporting real time joint force operations
Persistence	Conduct continuous ops; visit and revisit targets nearly at will	A function of airpower's speed and range	Distributed denial of service attacks (persist until deliberately and specifically countered)
Concentration	Concentrate overwhelming power at the right time and place	Airmen must guard against dilution of airpower	Simultaneous cyber attacks on or defense of multiple networks

Priority	Establish clear priorities for use of airpower	Demands for airpower may exceed available resources	Prioritized ISR feeds (reachback and "local")
Balance	Balance opportunity, necessity, effectiveness, and efficiency against risk to friendly forces	Cyberspace operations support other missions across the ROMO, giving commanders more capability and options to balance resources	Air Force networks can be used by Air Force members and other service, joint, interagency, non-governmental organizations and coalition military members (as necessary) to meet national security needs

INTEGRATION OF CYBERSPACE OPERATIONS ACROSS DOMAINS

The core of cross-domain integration is the ability to leverage capabilities from different domains to create unique—and often "decisive"—effects. As the use of cyberspace continues to evolve, Airmen will determine new ways to solve problems to meet national objectives.

The figure below portrays the relationship among the operational domains. This is important to consider because in modern warfare, all domains are interconnected via cyberspace operations.[22]

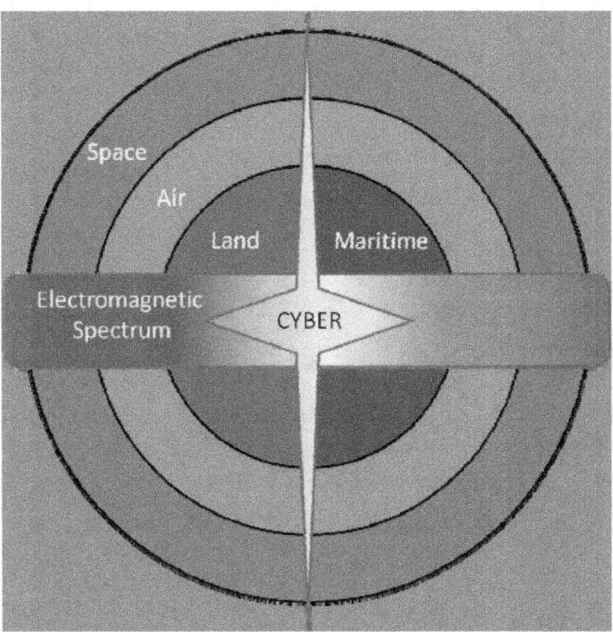

Figure 1.3. Warfighting Operational Domain Relationships

---

[22] Convertino, Sebastian, *Flying and Fighting in Cyberspace,* July 2007, Air University, p. 11.

CHAPTER TWO

COMMAND AND ORGANIZATION

We must treat our computers and networks similarly to our aircraft, satellites, and missiles. To this end, operations and maintenance will follow standards governed by a tight system of regulations and technical orders. Compliance with time critical software updates will gain new emphasis and commanders will be held accountable.

— General Norton A. Schwartz
Chief of Staff

POLICY RELATED TO COMMAND AND ORGANIZATION OF CYBERSPACE FORCES

According to the Deputy Secretary of Defense (DepSecDef), all combatant commands, military departments, and other defense components need the ability to operate unhindered in cyberspace; the domain does not fall within the purview of any one particular department or component. The Unified Command Plan assigns US Strategic Command (USSTRATCOM) the mission of synchronizing planning for cyberspace operations, in coordination with other combatant commanders (CCDRs), the Services, and, as directed, other US government agencies; and executing selected cyberspace operations. To support USSTRATCOM's cyberspace mission requirements, the commander of USSTRATCOM (CDRUSSTRATCOM) further delegated OPCON or TACON of designated cyber forces to the commander of US Cyber Command (CDRUSCYBERCOM).[23]

COMMAND RELATIONSHIPS

Command relationships are defined in JP 1, *Doctrine for the Armed Forces of the United States*. This guidance aims to establish and maintain unity of command, effort, and purpose in achieving joint force and national security objectives. Command relationships for specific operations are established in the governing operations order or execution order, and may vary from operation to operation. These SecDef-issued orders define supported and supporting relationships among the joint force commanders (JFCs).

---

[23] Derived from USCC CONOPS, dated 21 Sep 2010.

Combatant Command Support Relationships.[24] The geographic combatant commands (GCCs), US Central Command, US European Command, US Africa Command, US Southern Command, US Pacific Command (USPACOM), and US Northern Command (USNORTHCOM), are each assigned a geographic area of responsibility (AOR) within which their missions are accomplished with assigned and attached forces. Forces under the direction of the President or the SecDef may conduct operations from or within any geographic area as required for accomplishing assigned tasks, as mutually agreed by the CCDRs concerned or as specifically directed by the President or the SecDef.

Functional combatant commands (USSTRATCOM, US Transportation Command, and US Special Operations Command) support the GCCs, conduct operations in support of the President or the SecDef (normally in coordination with the GCC in whose AOR the operation will be conducted) and may be designated by the SecDef as the supported CCDR for some operations. When specialized units are assigned to functional CCDRs and one or more GCC wants those units for their operations, formal command relationships need to be established prior to initiation of operations. This applies to some cyberspace units. In these situations, GCCs are provided tailored support and forces by the CDRUSCYBERCOM depending on the type of contingency, the type of force requested, and what other operations are being conducted worldwide. There are several different command relationships available to ensure the GCC gets the capabilities and authorities needed to meet national objectives.

ORGANIZATION OF CYBERSPACE OPERATIONS

The Air Force organizes, trains, and equips its cyber forces to support the CCDRs and the joint warfighters, and to accomplish Service functions. Joint cyberspace forces are an integral part of military operations, and command relationships are crucial for ensuring timely and effective employment. CDRUSSTRATCOM advocates, plans, and executes military cyberspace operations and has the responsibility to prioritize, deconflict, integrate, and synchronize military cyberspace operations for current and planned joint operations. The Air Force presents some cyberspace forces to CDRUSSTRATCOM for day-to-day operations via its Service element, AFCYBER (24th Air Force). USNORTHCOM and USPACOM may conduct the civil support and homeland defense (HD) missions with cyberspace operations during critical infrastructure protection.[25] Like all Air Force forces, Air Force cyberspace forces may be assigned or attached to other CCDRs, coalition or joint force commanders, as directed.

---

[24] Adapted from JP 1, Executive Summary.
[25] See JP 3-27, *Homeland Defense,* 12 July 2007, p. 32.

United States Strategic Command (USSTRATCOM)

USSTRATCOM is responsible for synchronizing the planning of cyberspace operations.[26] The foundational command relationship for Air Force cyberspace forces under USSTRATCOM,[27] which:

- Directs global information grid (GIG) operations and defense.

- Plans against designated cyberspace threats.

- Coordinates with other combatant commands and appropriate US government agencies prior to the creation of cyberspace effects that cross AORs.

- Provides military representation to US national agencies, US commercial entities, and international agencies for matters related to cyberspace, as directed.

- Advocates for cyberspace capabilities

- Integrates theater security cooperation activities, deployments, and capabilities that support cyberspace operations, in coordination with the GCCs, and makes priority recommendations to the SecDef.

- Conducts operational preparation of the environment (OPE) and intelligence preparation of the operational environment (IPOE) and, as directed, synchronizes execution with GCCs.

- Executes cyberspace operations, as directed.

- Plans, coordinates, and executes kinetic and non-kinetic global strike as required.

Each of these missions assigned by the Unified Command Plan (UCP) has key functions, roles and responsibilities the Air Force accomplishes in order to support JFCs.

United States Cyber Command (USCYBERCOM)[28]

Mission: USCYBERCOM plans, coordinates, integrates, synchronizes, and conducts activities to direct the operations and defense of specified Department of Defense information networks and prepare to, and when directed, conduct full-spectrum

---

[26] The phrase "synchronizing planning" pertains specifically to planning efforts only and does not, by itself, convey authority to execute operations or direct execution of operations.
[27] Derived from the 2008 Unified Command Plan.
[28] Fact Sheets "USCYBERCOM" http://www.stratcom.mil/factsheets/Cyber_Command/

military cyberspace operations in order to enable actions in all domains, ensure US/allied freedom of action in cyberspace and deny the same to our adversaries.

Focus: USCYBERCOM fuses the Department's full spectrum of cyberspace operations and plans, coordinates, integrates, synchronizes, and conducts activities to lead day-to-day defense and protection of DOD information networks, coordinate DOD operations providing support to military missions, direct the operations and defense of specified DOD information networks, and prepare to, and when directed, conduct full spectrum military cyberspace operations. The command is charged with pulling together existing cyberspace resources and synchronizing warfighting effects to defend the information security environment.

USCYBERCOM centralizes command of cyberspace operations, strengthens DOD cyberspace capabilities, and integrates and bolsters the DOD's cyber expertise. USCYBERCOM's efforts support the Armed Services' ability to confidently conduct high-tempo, effective operations as well as protect command and control systems and the cyberspace infrastructure supporting weapons system platforms from disruptions, intrusions and attacks.

Forces: USCYBERCOM is a sub-unified command subordinate to USSTRATCOM. Service elements include:

USAF:	24th Air Force (AFCYBER)
USA:	Army Forces Cyber Command (ARCYBER)
USN:	Fleet Cyber Command (FLTCYBERCOM)
USMC:	Marine Forces Cyber Command (MARFORCYBER)

Air Force Space Command

AFSPC organizes, trains, and equips Air Force cyberspace forces to conduct sustained operations in, through, and from cyberspace and fully integrates with air and space operations. It serves as the lead major command (MAJCOM) for Air Force cyberspace procedures and concepts of operations. As the Air Force Service component commander to CDRUSSTRATCOM for Air Force cyberspace forces, the commander, AFSPC (AFSPC/CC) exercises administrative control (ADCON) over active component and specified elements of ADCON over activated reserve component Air Force cyber forces assigned or attached to USSTRATCOM. This includes those Air Force forces assigned or attached as part of USCYBERCOM under 24th Air Force (24 AF). Operational control (OPCON) over assigned and attached Air Force cyberspace forces will be as directed by CDRUSSTRATCOM, normally through CDRUSCYBERCOM to the commander, 24 AF (24 AF/CC). AFSPC supports all joint warfighters in the cyberspace domain by providing forces, through 24 AF, that establish, maintain, operate, and defend Air Force cyberspace components; exploit adversary vulnerabilities; attack adversary systems; and provide command and control for assigned and attached cyberspace forces.[29]

---

[29] AFSPC Cyberspace PAD, Change 4.

See AFDD 1, *Air Force Basic Doctrine, Organization, and Command*, for additional doctrinal guidance on ADCON and specified ADCON responsibilities.

24th Air Force

This numbered Air Force serves as the component numbered Air Force (C-NAF) to USCYBERCOM. In this role, the C-NAF commander serves as the senior Air Force warfighter for employment of assigned and attached forces under USCYBERCOM. As commander of Air Force forces (COMAFFOR), the 24 AF/CC is normally delegated OPCON of assigned and attached Air Force forces and exercises control via the 624th Operations Center (624 OC).

The 24 AF/CC is further responsible for executing Air Force Service tasks as directed by the Secretary of the Air Force and Chief of Staff of the Air Force (SECAF/CSAF) in the role as the commander, Air Force Network Operations (AFNETOPS/CC). These tasks include overseeing the morale, welfare, safety, and security of assigned and attached forces. They also include tasks inherent in the responsibility to provide, establish, and maintain a secure and defensible network in accordance with Air Force Guidance Memorandum 13-01. Per this document, the AFNETOPS/CC is "the single commander responsible for the overall operation, defense, maintenance and control of the AF-GIG."

Air Force Intelligence, Surveillance, and Reconnaissance Agency (AFISRA)

AFISRA is a field operating agency subordinate to the Deputy Chief of Staff, Intelligence, Surveillance, and Reconnaissance (AF/A2). AFISRA organizes, trains, equips, presents, and integrates all-source intelligence (e.g., signals intelligence [SIGINT], geospatial intelligence [GEOINT], measurement and signature intelligence, human intelligence, etc.) and full-spectrum capabilities to the intelligence community and to JFCs through the COMAFFOR. It provides customers at all echelons with multi-source intelligence products, applications, and services and provides intelligence expertise in the areas of SIGINT, IO (including information protection), acquisition, foreign weapons systems and technology, and treaty monitoring. In relation to cyberspace, AFISRA serves as the Air Force Service cryptologic component to the National Security Agency/Central Security Service (NSA/CSS), which authorizes SIGINT operations under Title 50, United States Code (U.S.C.). While NSA-derived analytic work roles are essential to cyber operations, employing full-spectrum cyber effects requires a multi-INT analysis approach. To enable 24 AF (AFCYBER) operations, AFISRA provides all-source cyber-focused ISR including digital network analysis to 24 AF through the 659th ISR Group. This support is generally characterized within five cyber-focused ISR areas: current intelligence and reporting, indications and warning, threat attribution and characterization, IPOE, and computer network exploitation.

COMMAND AND CONTROL OF CYBERSPACE FORCES

JP-1, *Doctrine for the Armed Forces of the United States,* defines generic models for command relationships under which forces may be assigned or attached. In all cases, the nature of the mission, forces, and overall objective should remain paramount in determining proper command relationships.

The JFC has the authority to organize assigned/attached forces to best accomplish the assigned mission based on the concept of operations (CONOPS). The JFC establishes subordinate commands, assigns responsibilities, establishes or delegates appropriate command relationships, and establishes coordinating instructions for subordinate commanders. When organizing joint forces, simplicity and clarity are critical.

See JP 1, *Doctrine for the Armed Forces of the United States*, and AFDD 1 for additional doctrinal guidance on command relationships.

C2 Options. When contemplating C2 options for joint cyberspace operations within the operational area, the JFC can choose to exercise C2 through the joint force staff, through a Service component commander, or through a functional component commander by designating one of the Service component commanders. Many factors will weigh on the JFC's selection, most notably the type and availability of forces/capabilities to accomplish the assigned mission. Additional factors may include host and friendly nation support, level and commitment of coalition forces, enemy capabilities and actions, and environmental limitations.

Theater-Level Considerations. When the GCC establishes a subordinate joint command to conduct operations, forces are normally attached as needed, with delegation of OPCON to the subordinate JFC. However, the GCC also will weigh the operational circumstances and decide if available cyberspace forces/capabilities can be most effectively employed by the subordinate JFC(s), by retaining them at the GCC level, or a combination thereof. This decision requires careful consideration after a thorough dialogue among the joint and Service component/force commanders.

Global Cyberspace Operations

Air Force cyberspace capabilities are used around the globe daily. The UCP establishes USSTRATCOM as the functional unified command with overall responsibility synchronizing planning for military cyberspace operations. CDRUSSTRATCOM exercises combatant command (command authority) (COCOM) of cyberspace forces assigned by the SecDef in the *Forces For Unified Commands* memorandum. CDRUSSTRATCOM has delegated OPCON to CDRUSCYBERCOM to employ these forces to support worldwide operations.

Some cyberspace capabilities require deconfliction with organizations outside assigned AORs due to collaboration with US government and partner nation organizations. Thus, theater and global cyberspace operations require a C2 system capable of collaborative design, planning, execution, and assessment across all affected AORs and with USSTRATCOM.

Cyberspace operations can be controlled as a global system operating as a single entity (for example, the Air Force portion of non-secure Internet Protocol Router Network), or by GCC's as part of theater operations. Global and theater cyberspace operations require different command relationships and levels of coordination to create desired effects.

Theater Cyberspace Integration

Cyberspace effects are created through the integration of cyberspace capabilities with air and space capabilities. The boundaries within which cyberspace C2 is exercised and the priorities and restrictions on its use should be identified in coordination with the JFC, non-DOD governmental agencies, and national leadership. The potential for cyberspace effects to cause strategically important consequences may often necessitate coordination with the highest levels of US and partner nation governments.

Theater commanders integrate cyberspace effects throughout joint and coalition military operations. Certain cyberspace forces move forward to conduct operations in specific theaters. Some organic cyberspace forces may also be assigned to particular theaters.

Even in the case of global functional C2, cyberspace experts normally are assigned to theater staffs to facilitate cyberspace integration. USSTRATCOM should provide representation to theater JFCs. For the Air Force, cyberspace expertise resides in each AOC. When requested to serve on theater staffs, the 24 AF presents expertise via an AF cyber liaison element to assist coordinating, deconflicting, synchronizing, and integrating global and theater cyberspace operations.

Air Force Presentation of Cyberspace Forces

Regional Organization and Control. In response to a military situation, a CCDR will normally organize a joint task force (JTF). If the entire theater is engaged, the CCDR may be the JFC. If the contingency is less than theater-wide, the CCDR may establish a subordinate JTF commanded by a subordinate JFC. In either case, the CCDR will first look to assigned in-theater forces. If augmentation is required, the JFC will request additional forces through the SecDef. Upon SecDef approval, additional forces will transfer into the theater and will be attached to the gaining CCDR, and the degree of control gained over those forces (i.e., OPCON or TACON) will be specified in the deployment orders. The gaining CCDR then normally delegates OPCON of these forces downward to the JTF commander who should, normally, delegate OPCON to the Service component commanders within the gaining JTF. All Air Force forces assigned or attached to a joint task force, or established as a single-Service task force, should be organized and presented as an Air Expeditionary Task Force (AETF).

○ Within a joint force, the JFC may organize forces in a mix of Service and functional components. All joint forces contain Service components, because administrative and logistical support for joint forces are provided through Service components.

Therefore, by definition, every joint force containing assigned or attached Air Force forces will have a COMAFFOR.

✪ The COMAFFOR normally exercises OPCON over Air Force forces within the AETF.

Functional Organization and Control. Not all air, space, and cyberspace forces employed in an operation will be attached forward to a geographic combatant commander. Some Air Force forces are capable of serving more than one GCC at a time. Such forces, such as inter-theater air mobility, space, and special operations forces, are organized under functional combatant commanders to facilitate optimal use of cross-AOR forces. When such forces are deployed in a GCC's AOR, they will often remain under the OPCON of their respective functional combatant commander and operate in support of the regional GCC. The SecDef establishes support relationships between the CCDRs for the planning and execution of joint operations.[30]

Normally, a support relationship is formally established between a GCC and USSTRATCOM. In some circumstances, after coordination with the owning commander and upon SecDef approval, control of functional forces may be transferred to a geographic commander with specification of OPCON or TACON.

OPCON over assigned and attached Air Force cyberspace forces will be as directed by CDRUSSTRATCOM, normally through CDRUSCYBERCOM to the 24 AF/CC. As the COMAFFOR, the 24 AF/CC normally exercises OPCON of assigned and attached Air Force forces through the 624th Operations Center (624 OC).

For more detailed information concerning presentation of forces, see AFDD 1, *Air Force Basic Doctrine, Organization, & Command.*

The JFC may elect to establish functional component commands to integrate specific capabilities across the joint force. The JFC normally appoints a joint force air component commander (JFACC) who is responsible for air effects within the theater. When the theater COMAFFOR is designated the JFACC, the COMAFFOR is prepared to command joint cyberspace forces as well as joint air forces since the JFC may also delegate authority for cyberspace effects to the JFACC. The JFC specifies the elements of TACON to be exercised over forces made available. Some cyberspace forces may be attached to a COMAFFOR/JFACC even though they may remain at home   station.

---

[30] JP 1, *Doctrine for the Armed Forces of the United States.*

CONSIDERATIONS ACROSS THE RANGE OF MILITARY OPERATIONS

Authorities and Legal / Law Enforcement Considerations and Constraints

Command, control, and organization of Air Force cyberspace forces are designed with inherent flexibility and versatility. These characteristics ensure Air Force cyberspace mission accomplishment across the range of military operations.

Legal considerations and international legal obligations apply to the employment of cyberspace capabilities. International law, domestic law and policy decisions, the law of armed conflict, and rules of engagement establish the legal framework within which operational activities are evaluated.

In certain situations, law enforcement authorities may be the driving forces for certain actions in military cyberspace operations. In these situations, law enforcement organizations (e.g., the Air Force Office of Special Investigation and Federal Bureau of Investigation) do three things: 1) make cases against criminals who represent a threat via cyberspace; 2) apprehend cyberspace criminals; and 3) preserve evidence of a cyberspace crime. The authority of cyberspace law enforcement agencies is driven by jurisdiction.

Mutually beneficial national interests govern coalition cyberspace force involvement. Coalition forces are integrated as needed and are tailored to each situation or operation based on the national interests of both the US and partner nations. The level of coalition integration is directly influenced by the partnerships or agreements made with the partner nation involved.

Across the range of military operations, cyberspace forces may at one moment be operating under authorities flowing from provisions of Title 10, U.S.C., *Armed Forces*, and another under Title 50, U.S.C., *War and National Defense.* In addition, Air National Guard cyberspace forces may be training under Title 32, U.S.C., *National Guard.* Guardsmen in Title 32 status may train for Title 10 missions but may not execute them. The rules for operating under these different titles of US law are very different and the authority to transition from one to another may be held at a very high level, even that of the President, although the individual conducting the operation and his/her immediate supervisors may be tactical-level "operators." It is important that individuals be clearly aware of the authority for each operation they are a part of, and the legal parameters that implies.

The employment of forces within this varied legal landscape emphasizes the need for clearly delineated command relationships. This is particularly true when reserve component forces (reserve or ANG) are being utilized. The authority that may be exercised varies with duty status and command relationships. Particular care should be given to clearly delineating command relationships that apply during various states of reserve component employment and training.

CHAPTER THREE

DESIGN, PLANNING, EXECUTION, AND ASSESSMENT

Although attacks in the cybersphere do not involve use of physical weapons, their destructive impacts, physical and otherwise, may be no less lethal to societies.

—Jeffrey R. Cooper,
Another View of Information Warfare

BASIC CONSIDERATIONS

Cyberspace operations may be conducted in a variety of situations and circumstances across the range of military operations. The decision of which cyberspace capabilities to employ is based not only on overall joint campaign or operation objectives, but on the risks of possible adversary responses and other potential second and third order effects on the campaign or operation.

Design of Cyberspace Operations

In cyberspace, the time between execution and effect can be milliseconds. Nonetheless, the observe-orient-decide-act (OODA) loop remains a valid construct for examining the decision cycle in cyberspace. Ongoing operations can be considered those operations that span past the phases of warfare.

Even for ongoing operations, planning at the strategic level is imperative because cyberspace operations can create effects simultaneously at the strategic, operational, and tactical levels across multiple domains. Planners should provide inputs to and receive feedback from appropriate intelligence and targeting organizations across the full range of government organizations and partner nations. Cyberspace's unique attributes and potential for speed require the ability to react to rapidly changing situations.

Inclusion of cyberspace superiority strategy in formal planning normally offers many planning and execution options to meet a theater JFC's objectives. Cyberspace operations can enable creation of many effects that formerly required physical attack to accomplish. Descriptions of these processes can be found in JP 5-0, *Joint Operation Planning*.

Planning

Airmen should be prepared to articulate to commanders the advantages that cyberspace operations can provide, as well as the dangers of unintended and undesirable effects and the need for close coordination between the many agencies with a role in cyberspace operations. Cyberspace operations normally are planned as part of major operations and campaigns, homeland operations, crisis response, and limited contingency operations. In these cases, planning is normally fully integrated into the joint operations planning process at the JFC level and in the joint operations planning process (JOPP) at the component level.

Security versus Capability

Planners should consider the impact of increasing security in cyberspace on operations. Changing information operations conditions or deploying additional tools to analyze networks can cause slower network operation speeds. In a bandwidth-limited environment or in an environment with many dispersed forces, planners should account for impacts of how measures designed to improve cyberspace defenses could actually hinder or desynchronize operations.

Logistics Support

Readiness and sustainability of cyberspace capabilities are directly related to the quality of logistics planning. Cyberspace logistics programs should be developed in balance with modernization efforts and the operating capability each category of resources provides. Emphasis should be on total effectiveness to maximize cyberspace operations capabilities.

Execution

During the execution stage across the range of military operations, cyberspace operators within the AOC will integrate cyberspace effects into the COMAFFOR/JFACC's time-phased scheme of maneuver and fires based on commander's guidance, desired effects, friendly capabilities, and likely adversary courses of action. USSTRATCOM cyberspace support may be obtained through the supported/supporting relationship and should be fully integrated into the COMAFFOR/JFACC's planning and execution.

Global Operations

The tasking cycle for cyberspace operations is the process the 624 OC uses to translate CDRUSCYBERCOM and theater JFC's objectives, priorities, and intent into a coherent, executable plan for Air Force cyberspace forces. The 624 OC's process is a derivative of the Joint Operations Planning Process–Air (JOPP-A). The Air Force cyber tasking order (CTO), a key product of the tasking cycle, is used to task and execute assigned and attached cyberspace forces. The cyber tasking order is analogous to an air tasking order. The cyber tasking cycle, which is based on the air tasking cycle, is an iterative process for planning, coordinating, apportioning, allocating, executing, and assessing the effectiveness of cyberspace operations. The cycle can be lengthened or shortened to synchronize with the theater battle rhythm to support crisis. It includes continuous collection, correlation, and prioritization of many inputs to meet CDRUSCYBERCOM and theater JFC's intent and objectives.

The CTO is derived from CDRUSCYBERCOM orders and, when supported, JFC's orders. It tasks assigned and attached cyberspace forces, provides guidance for synchronization of global and theater joint air, space, and cyberspace operations, and provides special instructions for the period it covers. Every cyberspace operation during that period should be on the CTO for situational awareness and deconfliction purposes.

Theater Operations

The air and space tasking cycles are the processes the theater AOC uses to translate JFC objectives, priorities, and intent into a coherent, executable plan for assigned and attached Air Force forces. The air operations directive and the air tasking order (ATO) are key products of the air and space tasking cycle.

The joint air and space operations plan reflects the COMAFFOR/JFACC's integrated air, space, and cyberspace operations plan to support the JFC's campaign. It should include the tasking of all assigned or attached cyberspace forces and all requests for theater support from global cyberspace forces. Air Force cyberspace forces that are assigned or attached with specification of OPCON or TACON to a theater COMAFFOR/JFACC are integrated into operations via the air tasking cycle and tasked via the ATO.

Integration and Synchronization of Theater and Global Operations

When the 624 OC is supporting a theater operation, the CTO is synchronized with the theater ATO throughout the tasking cycle, with theater operators working closely with those at the 624 OC. If supporting a single, primary theater, the tasking cycle is synchronized with that theater's tasking cycle to optimize cyberspace support to the theater. The 624 OC, using guidance from the COMAFFOR/JFACC, helps develop cyberspace courses of action in support of theater operations. During the planning phase, the 624 OC uses COMAFFOR/JFACC guidance, rules of engagement (ROE), the joint integrated prioritized target list, the target nomination list, and the approved master air attack plan (MAAP), to finalize the CTO. After the ATO is finalized, the theater AOC forwards it to all required users to include the 624 OC. During execution, cyberspace tasking can occur dynamically to meet supported commander's requests.

Assessment

Assessment encompasses efforts, at all levels of conflict, use logical and defensible constructs to evaluate effects, gauge progress toward accomplishment of actions and objectives, and make strategy recommendations to shape future action. Assessments of operations conducted in and through cyberspace follow the same general procedures as the assessment of all other operations and are informed by a range of inputs, including ISR, munitions effectiveness, and operational reporting.

There are two primary types of assessments accomplished at the operational level, tactical and operational-level. Tactical assessment (TA) is generally performed by the AOC's ISR division and focuses on the effectiveness of tactical operations. Operational-level assessment (OA) of strategy is usually executed within the strategy division, provides insights and recommendations on the relevant commander's (i.e., COMAFFOR/JFACC or 24 AF/CC) strategy.

Tactical Assessment (TA)

TA is the overall determination of the effectiveness of tactical operations. It consists of the evaluation of tactical actions against assigned tactical tasks using empirical, objective, and usually quantifiable measures for collection and analysis. TA analysts collect, aggregate, analyze, and archive relevant data. This level of assessment determines commander need to take further tactical action. TA answers such questions as: "Was the intended action accomplished?," "Was the intended direct effect created?," "Has the target's status changed?," and "Is re-engagement, re-attack, or 're-influence' necessary?"

To make assessment most effective, measures and indicators should be determined during the planning process. TA of an operation is based on post-mission analysis. Task accomplishment and resulting potential direct effects are measured through a variety of intelligence and analytical methods, including SIGINT and GEOINT, among other means.

Indirect effects, such as potential changes in behavior that are very difficult to assess in a time-sensitive manner, are best assessed at the operational level and above.

Operational-Level Assessment (OA)

OA assessment is an analytically supported judgment of a commander's strategy (ends, ways and means). This type of assessment is the first level at which complex indirect effects are normally evaluated, progress toward operational and strategic objectives is measured, and recommendations for strategy adjustments and future action extending beyond re-attack are made.

Assessment at the operational level focuses on both effects and performance via measures of effectiveness (MOE) and measures of performance (MOP), respectively. MOEs are "used to assess changes in system behavior, capability, or operational environment that is tied to measuring the attainment of an end state, achievement of an objective, or creation of an effect."[31] MOPs are "used to assess friendly actions that [are] tied to measuring task accomplishment."[32] In short, MOEs help measure progress toward the end state while MOPs are used to measure the strategy's ways and means. These measures should flow from the development of criteria that define the conditions required to receive specific assessment grades. This grading of the strategy's ends,

---

[31] JP 3-0
[32] Ibid.

ways, and means is often presented using a stoplight chart – with specific criteria designated for red, yellow, and green – in order to yield consistent, meaningful, and understandable feedback to the commander.

In order to accomplish this assessment process within the interrelated and complex nature of many cyberspace operations, operational-level cyberspace planners and analysts should develop an intimate understanding of the linkage between cyberspace and the supported mission or operation. This requires direct feedback from those closest to observing the intended effects, such as the Airmen executing cyber-enabled Air Force missions or the warfighters in theater, in order to assess the level of cyberspace performance and effectiveness. For example, the assessment of cyberspace operational effects in support of influence operations requires an in-depth understanding of the warfighter's desired impact on behavior and the ability to measure any resulting behavioral changes.

Situation Reporting

In addition to the assessment provided by the strategy team regarding conduct of combat operations, the COMAFFOR/JFACC and 24 AF/CC should receive daily reports on the status of friendly forces. Commanders should prioritize assets by their criticality to operations and have situational awareness of their linkages in the domain. In addition, they should anticipate cascading effects of degraded operations similar to attacks on assets in other domains. Additionally, the 24 AF/CC should ensure situation reporting is operationally-focused and addresses enemy actions and attacks, friendly actions taken to mitigate threats, and subsequent impact on friendly forces.

AUTHORITIES AND LEGAL CONSIDERATIONS

Authorities

Cyberspace forces will normally conduct operations under the authority of Title 10 or Title 50. The authorities invoked will differ depending on the type of operation being conducted. The rules for operating under these varying titles are different. Authorities to act against adversaries are included in the execute order or operation order for a specific operation. If aggressive defensive responses or counter-offensive operations are authorized, authorities should be clearly defined and understood. Cyberspace forces belonging to the Air National Guard are governed in peacetime by Title 32.

Legal Considerations

Cyberspace operations may be conducted at any level of war and, within legal parameters, across the entire range of military operations in support of global and theater objectives.

Legal considerations and international legal obligations apply to the employment of cyberspace capabilities. International law, domestic law and policy decisions, the law of armed conflict, and rules of engagement establish the legal framework within which operational activities are evaluated. Usually, the staff judge advocate on a commander's staff advises the given commander on the lawful means of conducting cyberspace operations as detailed in JP 1-04, *Legal Support to Military Operations*. Sound legal advice throughout the planning and execution of cyberspace operations is essential to mission success. This is especially important while courses of action are being developed and before they are executed. Early identification of legal issues will maximize planning efforts by developing lawful courses of action early in the planning process. The legal support staff should have access (billets and clearances) to the information, processes, and programs used in cyberspace operations and understanding of the underlying cyber technologies.

CONSIDERATIONS ACROSS THE RANGE OF MILITARY OPERATIONS

Engagement and Cooperation Operations

Multinational operations are becoming the norm for military operations, making intelligence and information sharing with allies and coalition partners increasingly important. Connectivity is essential, particularly when the US, allies, and coalition host nation forces function in mutual support during combat operations. Interoperability issues should also be considered in light of the Air Force's need for information assurance. As a part of a larger networked team, the Air Force should plan and execute in complete concert with other Services, nations, and agencies.

Homeland Operations

Cyberspace capabilities play a major role in homeland operations (e.g., disaster relief) when they are needed to rebuild portions of the cyberspace domain or to restore access to the domain. Timely and coordinated US government responses are important when establishing and reconstituting cyberspace capabilities.

Attack and exploitation operations in an HD scenario may involve complex legal and policy issues; however, these issues do not prevent the application of attack and exploitation operations for HD, but temper it. Unless approved by appropriate authorities, DOD assets cannot be used to perform attack or exploit operations on US entities. Also, information sharing protocols, laws, and policies regulate, and at times may prevent, data and information sharing between agencies, organizations, and nations, thereby potentially reducing knowledge development. Protection of classified and sensitive information may also preclude effective sharing with other agencies and coalition partners

Establishing the Cyberspace Infrastructure in Afghanistan

In 2007, in support of Operation ENDURING FREEDOM, the 3rd Combat Communication Group (3 CCG) deployed to Kabul, Afghanistan and established an Enterprise Network for Afghanistan's Ministry of Interior (MoI) which provides capabilities such as e-mail, telephone service through "voice over Internet protocol" and video teleconferencing capability between the National Police Coordination Center, six joint regional coordination centers, 12 Kabul headquarters buildings, 38 provincial command centers as well as about 200 other locations such as medical and fire stations. Also, 3 CCG provided the infrastructure to allow network technicians to protect MoI's computers against viruses and provided a platform from which they can defend against cyber-attack.

Properly implemented cyberspace operations support defense of the homeland. When a domestic incident occurs, the escalation processes inherent in civil support procedures are implemented. A non-DOD civilian agency is in charge of civil support incidents, and military assistance is provided through a relationship similar to direct support, as articulated in civil support agreements and the Standing civil support EXORD. In all cases, the Air Force is prepared to support homeland operations through intelligence and information sharing within the appropriate legal framework.

Reconstituting the Cyberspace Infrastructure during Disaster Relief

In 2005, the US's Gulf of Mexico region was devastated by a hurricane which destroyed critical infrastructure in Mississippi, Louisiana, and Texas. This disaster displaced tens of thousands of people seeking to escape the impact of the storm. Based on their expertise for extending the cyberspace domain, Air Force combat communications groups deployed throughout the Gulf region to reconstitute the cyberspace domain and allow military and US government organizations to communicate and be connected for situational awareness and C2.

Crisis Response and Limited Contingency Operation Considerations

These missions may be operations into friendly nations; however, some states are unstable and may include elements that are actively hostile toward the US. In other situations, political or international considerations may require air operations to be conducted within known threat areas. Cyberspace forces may or may not have to deploy to support these operations.

Major Operations and Campaigns

In addition to other ongoing missions, cyberspace operations can be planned as part of major operations and campaigns. In these cases, planning should be fully integrated into the joint operation planning process at the JFC level and the joint operations planning process for Air at the component level. Descriptions of these processes can be found in JP 5-0, *Joint Operation Planning*, and AFDD 3-0, *Operations and Planning*. This kind of operational planning does not significantly differ from planning for operations in other domains in terms of processes, thus this section concentrates upon the continuous, cyclic, and iterative nature of ongoing cyberspace operations.

Inclusion of a strategy for cyberspace superiority in formal planning offers commanders many "non-traditional" options. Cyberspace operations enable creation of effects that formerly required physical attack to accomplish. Cyberspace operations also open avenues for exploitation of adversary capabilities and for changing the information that the adversary receives. This type of effect may not be possible through access in the other physical domains.

During the execution stage of major operations and campaigns, cyberspace planners and operators should work in conjunction with the COMAFFOR's time-phased scheme of maneuver for a given tasking period. Planners should synthesize commander's guidance, desired effects, supported components' schemes of maneuver, friendly capabilities, and likely adversary courses of action. Operators will employ friendly resources against approved targets.

CONCLUSION

Cyberspace operations are evolving inside the DOD and the Air Force. Air Force Space Command and 24 AF form the foundation of Air Force cyberspace operations. Their resulting capabilities support all geographic and functional combatant commanders. This doctrine document establishes fundamentals for Air Force cyberspace operations. Uses of the cyberspace domain continue to evolve as new concepts and capabilities are developed. The Air Force recognizes its critical dependence on cyberspace. Hence, a culture shift is underway that reflects the reality that cyberspace is a contested domain and the importance of maintaining cyberspace superiority.

The Air Force will develop unique cyber capabilities that originate in its distinct missions and take full advantage of the integration of air, space, and cyber capabilities. Each Service brings its own cyber strengths and capabilities to the joint team and the nation. Since air, space, and cyberspace are inextricably linked, the potential exists to integrate capabilities across these domains to exponentially increase each other's power. This integration promises to give joint force commanders unrivaled global access, persistence, awareness and connectivity capabilities and to rapidly restore critical infrastructure via a cross-domain network-of-networks approach. The Air Force seeks to develop cyberspace capabilities that complement those of other services and will explore the combination of cyberspace with other non-kinetic capabilities to achieve synergies.

The Air Force's growing reliance on cyberspace requires a well-educated and trained professional cadre composed of cyberspace operators and leaders who are ready to provide the required capability and capacity for mission accomplishment. Professional cyberspace operators with technical and tactical expertise are mission essential individuals. Experience shows us that cyberspace operators should possess high levels of technical competence, robust analytical skills, and a critical understanding of cyberspace warfare application. Finally, this professional corps should take advantage of experience and skill sets from multiple existing Air Force specialties and be represented across the total force structure.

Each Airman should be an educated and responsible user of cyberspace capabilities. We should take care of each other as good wingmen in cyberspace.

AT THE VERY HEART OF WARFARE LIES DOCTRINE...

APPENDIX A – TEN THINGS EVERY AIRMAN MUST KNOW

1. The United States is vulnerable to cyberspace attacks by relentless adversaries attempting to infiltrate our networks at work and at home – millions of times a day, 24/7.

2. Our adversaries plant malicious code, worms, botnets, and hooks in common websites, software, and hardware such as thumbdrives, printers, etc.

3. Once implanted, this code begins to distort, destroy, and manipulate information, or "phone" it home. Certain code allows our adversaries to obtain higher levels of credentials to access highly sensitive information.

4. The adversary attacks your computers at work and at home knowing you communicate with the Air Force network by email or by transferring information from one system to another.

5. As cyber wingmen, you have a critical role in defending your networks, your information, your security, your teammates, and your country.

6. You significantly decrease our adversaries' access to our networks, critical Air Force information, and even your personal identity by taking simple action.

7. Do not open attachments or click on links unless the email is digitally signed, or you can directly verify the source—even if it appears to be from someone you know.

8. Do not connect any hardware or download any software, applications, music, or information onto our networks without approval.

9. Encrypt sensitive but unclassified and/or critical information. Ask your computer security administrator for more information.

10. Install the free Department of Defense anti-virus software on your home computer. Your computer security administrator can provide you with your free copy.

— **Gen Norton A. Schwartz,**
Chief of Staff, US Air Force
"Defending Our Networks and Our Country"

APPENDIX B – POLICY AND DOCTRINE RELATED TO CYBERSPACE OPERATIONS

MATRIX OF CYBERSPACE OPERATIONS DOCUMENTS	
National-Level Documents	
National Security Strategy	The National Security Strategy of the United States of America is a document prepared periodically by the executive branch of the government of the United States for congress that outlines the major national security concerns of the United States and how the administration plans to deal with them. The legal foundation for the document is spelled out in the Goldwater-Nichols Act. The document is purposely general in content (contrast with the National Military Strategy) and its implementation relies on elaborating guidance provided in supporting documents (including the National Military Strategy [NMS]).
US *National Strategy to Secure Cyberspace*, February 2003	Covers the necessity for vigilance in cyberspace, many defensive aspects of cyberspace operations, and the general principles that should guide national response to a cyberspace "crisis."[33]
Department of Defense Documents	
National Defense Strategy (NDS)	The NDS is issued periodically and the last one was published in June 2008. It outlines how the Department supports the President's National Security Strategy and informs the National Military Strategy and other subordinate strategy documents. The strategy builds on lessons learned and insights from previous operations and strategic reviews such as the 2006 Quadrennial Defense Review.
National Military Strategy	The NMS is issued by the Chairman of the Joint Chiefs of Staff as a deliverable to the Secretary of Defense briefly outlining the strategic aims of the armed Services. The NMS's chief source of guidance is the National Security Strategy document. The Chairman of the Joint Chiefs of Staff, in consultation with the other members of the Joint Chiefs of Staff, the Commanders of the Unified Combatant Commands, the Joint Staff, and the Office of the Secretary of Defense, prepares the National Military Strategy in accordance with 10 U.S.C., Section 153. Title 10 requires that not later than February 15 of each even-numbered year, the Chairman submit to the Senate Committee on Armed Services and the House Committee on Armed Services a comprehensive examination of the national military

---

[33] *National Strategy for Securing Cyberspace*, The White House, February 2003.

	strategy. This report must delineate a national military strategy consistent with the most recent National Security Strategy prescribed by the President; the most recent annual report of the Secretary of Defense submitted to the President and Congress; and the most recent Quadrennial Defense Review conducted by the Secretary of Defense.
National Military Strategy for Cyberspace Operations (NMS-CO), December 2006	The NMS-CO describes the cyberspace domain, articulates cyberspace threats and vulnerabilities, and provides a strategic framework for action. The NMS-CO is the US Armed Forces' comprehensive strategic approach for using cyberspace operations to assure US military strategic superiority in the domain. The integration of offensive and defensive cyberspace operations, coupled with the skill and knowledge of our people, is fundamental to this approach.
Unified Command Plan (UCP) 6 April 2011	The UCP assigns USSTRATCOM the mission of synchronizing planning for cyberspace operations, in coordination with other CCDRs, the Services, and, as directed, other US government agencies; and executing selected cyberspace operations.
Joint Operations Planning and Execution System (JOPES)	The JOPES is the Department of Defense's (DOD's) principal means for translating national security policy decisions into military plans and operations. JOPES Functional Managers grant permissions, restrict access to operation plans on the database, and perform periodic reviews of user IDs and the content of the JOPES database to ensure outdated plans and accounts are removed when no longer required.
CJCS Net-Centric Operational Environment (NCOE) Joint Integrating Concept (JIC) v1 31 Oct 2005	This document provides a conceptual look at how the NCOE will enhance the overall performance of warfighters at every level. Its focus is supporting a JTF, including the JTF commander, JTF mission partners, and warfighters at the "first tactical mile." The goal is for the entire joint force and mission partners to have the technical connectivity and interoperability necessary to rapidly and dynamically share knowledge amongst decision-makers, communities of interest, and others, while protecting information from those who should not have it—all to facilitate the coherent application of joint action. The NCOE will translate information superiority into combat power by effectively linking (both horizontally and vertically) knowledgeable entities throughout the battlespace, thus making possible dramatically new ways of operating and, by extension, decisive advantages in warfighting. The timeframe is 8 to 20 years in the future, with an illustrative focus on the year 2015.
DOD Directive 3600.01, *Information Operations*, 23 May	Covers some of the computer network aspects of cyberspace operations, classifying them as part of IO. 3600.01 discusses "computer network operations," comprised of "computer network

MATRIX OF CYBERSPACE OPERATIONS DOCUMENTS	
2011 (Secret; title and information extracted are unclassified)	attack," computer network defense," and computer network exploitation," but does not discuss networks or cyberspace operations in a more holistic sense. Some further guidance may be found in the NMS-CO, but the details are not releasable at this time.
SecDef Memorandum, *Command and Control for Military Cyberspace Missions*, 12 November 2008,	Specifies that USSTRATCOM's JTF-GNO falls under the operational control of USSTRATCOM's USCYBERCOM, which directly impacts the organization of the global functional combatant command responsible for much joint cyberspace activity.
DODD 3020.40, *Defense Critical Infrastructure Program* (DCIP), 14 January 2010	This Directive cancels DOD Directive 5160.54, "Critical Asset Assurance Program," January 20, 1998 (hereby canceled), updates policy, and assigns responsibilities for the DCIP, incorporating guidance from the President in Homeland Security Presidential Directive #7, December 17, 2003 to function as the Sector-Specific Agency for the Defense Industrial Base with the following responsibilities: collaborate with all relevant Federal departments and agencies, State and local governments, and the private sector, including with key persons and entities in their infrastructure sector; conduct or facilitate vulnerability assessments of the sector and encourage risk management strategies to protect against and mitigate the effects of attacks against critical infrastructure and key resources. This Directive cancels Deputy Secretary of Defense Memorandum, "Critical Infrastructure Protection Responsibilities and Realignments," August 11, 1999 (hereby canceled) and supersedes The Department of Defense Critical Infrastructure Protection Plan, November 18, 1998 (hereby superseded), and the Deputy Secretary of Defense Memorandum, "Realignment of Critical Infrastructure Protection Oversight to the Assistant Secretary of Defense for Homeland Defense," September 3, 2003 (hereby superseded).
DODD 3020.26, *Department of Defense Continuity Programs*, January 9, 2009	DOD policy that all defense continuity-related activities, programs, and requirements of the DOD Components, including those related to continuity of operations, continuity of government, and enduring constitutional Government, shall ensure the continuation of current approved DOD and DOD component mission essential functions all circumstances across the spectrum of threats
•DODD 8500.01E, *Information Assurance*, 24	Establishes policy and assigns responsibilities to achieve Department of Defense (DOD) information assurance (IA) through a defense-in-depth approach that integrates the

MATRIX OF CYBERSPACE OPERATIONS DOCUMENTS

October 2002	capabilities of personnel, operations, and technology, and supports the evolution to network centric warfare
•DODD O-8530.01 *Computer Network Defense*, 1 January 2001	Establishes policy, definition, and responsibilities for CND within DOD information systems and computer networks
DODI O-3600.02 *Information Operations Security Classification Guidance*, 28 Nov 1995	Provides DOD-level security classification guidance relevant to some cyberspace operations
DODI 8410.02, *Network Operations for the GIG*, 19 Dec 08	Incorporates and cancels DOD chief information officer Guidance and Policy Memoranda No. 10-8460 and No. 4-8460. Establishes policy and assigns responsibilities for implementing and executing NetOps, the DOD-wide operational, organizational, and technical capabilities for operating and defending the GIG. Institutionalizes NetOps as an integral part of the GIG
DODI O-8530.02 *Support to Computer Network Defense*, 9 Mar 2001	Implements policy, assigns responsibilities, and prescribes procedures under DODD 8530.01
JP 1, *Doctrine for the Armed Forces of the United States*, 14 May 2007, Change 1 20 March 2009	This publication is the capstone joint doctrine publication. It provides doctrine for unified action by the Armed Forces of the United States. As such, it specifies the authorized command relationships and authority that military commanders can use, provides guidance for the exercise of that military authority, provides fundamental principles and guidance for command and control, prescribes guidance for organizing joint forces, and describes policy for selected joint activities. It also provides the doctrinal basis for interagency coordination and for US military involvement in multiagency and multinational operations.
JP 2-0, *Joint Intelligence*, 22 June 2007	This publication is the keystone document of the joint intelligence series. It provides fundamental principles and guidance for intelligence support to joint operations and unified action.
JP 2-01, *Joint and National Intelligence Support to Military Operations*, 07 October 2004	This publication establishes doctrinal guidance on the provision of joint and national intelligence products, services, and support to military operations.
JP 2-01.3, *Joint Intelligence*	This publication describes the process in which the adversary and other relevant aspects of the operational environment are

MATRIX OF CYBERSPACE OPERATIONS DOCUMENTS

Preparation of the Operational Environment, 16 June 2009	analyzed to identify possible adversary courses of action and to support joint operation planning, execution, and assessment.
JP 3-0, *Joint Operations*, 11 August 2011	This publication is the keystone document of the joint operations series. It provides the doctrinal foundation and fundamental principles that guide the Armed Forces of the United States in the conduct of joint operations across the range of military operations.
JP 3-08, *Interagency, Intergovernmental Organization, and Nongovernmental Organization Coordination During Joint Operations Vol I and II*, 17 March 2006	Volume I discusses the interagency, intergovernmental organization (IGO), and nongovernmental organization (NGO) environment and provides fundamental principles and guidance to facilitate coordination between the Department of Defense, and other US Government agencies, IGOs, NGOs, and regional organizations. Volume II describes key US Government departments and agencies, IGOs and NGOs — their core competencies, basic organizational structures, and relationship, or potential relationship, with the Armed Forces of the United States.
JP 3-13, *Information Operations*, 13 February 2006	This publication provides doctrine for information operations planning, preparation, execution, and assessment in support of joint operations.
JP 3-13.1, *Electronic Warfare*, 25 January 2007	This publication provides joint doctrine for electronic warfare planning, preparation, execution, and assessment in support of joint operations across the range of military operations.
JP 3-13.3, *Operations Security*, 29 June 2006	This publication provides doctrine for planning, preparation, execution, and assessment of operations security in joint operations.
JP 3-13.4, *Military Deception*, 13 July 2006	This publication provides joint doctrine for the planning and execution of military deception at the combatant command and/or subordinate joint force level.
JP 3-14, *Space Operations*, 6 January 2009	This publication provides joint doctrine for planning, executing, and assessing joint space operations.
JP 3-13.2 *Psychological Operations*, 0707 January 2010	This publication addresses military psychological operations planning and execution in support of joint, multinational, and interagency efforts across the range of military operations
JP 5-0, *Joint Operation Planning* 11 August 2011	This publication is the keystone doctrine for joint operation planning throughout the range of military operations.
JP 6-0, *Joint Communications System*, 10 June	This publication is the keystone document for the communications system series of publications. This publication presents approved doctrine for communications system support

MATRIX OF CYBERSPACE OPERATIONS DOCUMENTS	
2010	to joint and multinational operations and outlines the responsibilities of Services, agencies, and combatant commands with respect to ensuring effective communications system support to commanders.
Air Force-Level Documents	
HQ USAF Program Action Directive 07-08 (Change 4), *Phase I of Implementation of Secretary of Air Force Direction to Organize Air Force Cyberspace Forces*, 20 February 2009	Organization of the Air Force's Service contribution to cyberspace operations.
AFDD 1, *Air Force Basic Doctrine, Organization, and Command*, 14 October 2011	This document is the premier statement of US Air Force basic doctrine. It has been prepared under the direction of the CSAF. It establishes general doctrinal guidance for the application of air and space forces in operations across the full range of military operations
AFDD 3-0, *Operations and Planning*, 3 April 2007	This document has been prepared under the direction of the CSAF. It establishes doctrinal guidance for organizing, planning, and employing air, space, and cyberspace forces at the operational level of conflict across the full range of military operations. It is the capstone of US Air Force operational-level doctrine publications. Together, these publications collectively form the basis from which commanders plan and execute their assigned air and space missions and their actions as a component of a joint Service or multinational force.
AFDD 3-13, *Information Operations*, 11 January 2005	This AFDD establishes doctrinal guidance for information operations. More detailed doctrinal discussions of information operations concepts are explained in AFDD 3-13.1, *Electronic Warfare Operations*; and AFDD 3-61, *Public Affairs Operations*. The nomenclature of these publications is subject to change. Other AFDDs also discuss information operations as they apply to those specific airpower functions.
AFDD 3-61, *Public Affairs*, 23 December 2010	This document articulates fundamental Air Force principles for conducting public affairs operations and provides commanders with operational-level guidance for employing and integrating those capabilities across the range of air, space, and information operations.

REFERENCES

Air Force Publications

(NOTE: all AFDDs are available at HTTP://WWW.E-PUBLISHING.AF.MIL)

AFDD 1, *Air Force Basic Doctrine, Organization and Command*
AFDD 3-0, *Operations and Planning*
AFDD 3-01, *Air Warfare*
AFDD 3-24, *Irregular Warfare*
AFDD 4-0, *Combat Support*
AFDD 3-13, *Information Operations*
AFDD 3-13.1, *Electronic Warfare*
AFDD 3-61, *Public Affairs Operations*
AFDD 6-0, *Command and Control Systems*

Joint Publications

CJCSM 6510.01, Defense-in-Depth: Information Assurance (IA) and Computer Network Defense (CND)
CJCSI 5120.02B, Joint Doctrine Development Systems
CM-0527-08, Definition of Cyberspace Operations
SM 183-06, Joint Concept of Operations for Global Information Grid NetOps
JP 1, *Doctrine for the Armed Forces of the United States*
JP 2-0, *Joint Intelligence*
JP 3-0, *Joint Operations*
JP 3-08, *Interagency, Intergovernmental Organization, and Nongovernmental Organization Coordination During Joint Operations Vol I & II*
JP 3-13, *Information Operations*
JP 3-13.1, *Electronic Warfare*
JP 3-13.2, *Psychological Operations*
JP 3-13.3, *Operations Security*
JP 3-13.4, *Military Deception*
JP 3-14, *Space Operations*
JP 3-30, *Command and Control for Joint Air Operations*
JP 3-60, *Joint Targeting*
JP 5-0, *Joint Operation Planning*
JP 6-0, *Joint Communications System*

National and DOD Publications

Unified Command Plan (UCP), 6 April 2011
National Security Presidential Directive (NSPD)-54, Cyberspace Security, 8 January 2008
National Military Strategy for Cyberspace Operations (NMS-CO), 11 December 2006

DepSecDef Memo, *The Definition of "Cyberspace"*, 12 May 2008
DODD 3020.40, Defense *Critical Infrastructure Program (DCIP)*, 14 January 2010
DODD 3020.26, *Department of Defense Continuity Programs*, January 9, 2009.
DODD 3100.10, *Space Policy*, 9 July 1999
DODD O-5100.30, *Department of Defense Command and Control*, 5 Jan 2006
DODD 8100.01, *Global Information Grid Overarching Policy*, 21 Nov 03
DODD O-8530.1, *Computer Network Defense (CND)*, 8 January 2001
DODI S-3100.15, *Space Control*, 19 January 2001
DODI 4650.01, *Policy and Procedures for Management and Use of the Electromagnetic Spectrum*, 9 January 2009
DODI 8410.02, *NetOps for the Global Information Grid (GIG)*, 19 December 2008
DODI O-8530.2, *Support to Computer Network Defense (CND)*, 9 March 2001

Other Publications

US Army Field Manual 3-13, *Information Operations*, 28 November 2003
US Army Field Manual 3-05.30, *Psychological Operations*, April 2005
Field Manual 3-05.301, *Psychological Operations Process Tactics, Techniques, and Procedures*, August 2007
US Army Field Manual 3-05.302, *Tactical Psychological Operations, Tactics, Techniques, and Procedures*, April 2005
Navy Warfare Publication 3-13, *Navy Information Operations*, June 2003
Navy Warfare Publication 3-63, Vol. I, *Computer Network Operations*, January 2008
Navy Warfare Publication 3-63, Vol. II, *Computer Network Operations*, September 2008
Navy Tactics, Techniques, and Procedures 3-13.1, *Theater and Campaign Information Operations Planning*, January 2008
Navy Tactics, Techniques, and Procedures 3-13.2, *Navy Information Operations Warfare Commander's Manual*, May 2006
Marine Corps Warfighting Publication 3-40.4, *Marine Air-Ground Task Force Information Operations*, 9 July 2003
Allied Joint Publication 3-10, *Allied Joint Doctrine for Information Operations*, 2006
Playbook for Cyberspace Intrusions, 28 May 2008

Chief of Staff of the Air Force (CSAF Professional Reading Program)

The CSAF's professional reading list with book reviews is available on the Air Force web site at: http://www.af.mil/information/csafreading/index.asp. The list is subject to revision. Readers are encouraged to check the Air Force web site (http://www.af.mil) for   the   most   current   information.

GLOSSARY

Abbreviations and Acronyms

AETF	air expeditionary task force
AFDD	Air Force Doctrine Document
AFISRA	Air Force Intelligence, Surveillance, and Reconnaissance Agency
AFSPC	Air Force Space Command
AJP	allied joint publication
AOC	air and space operations center
AOR	area of responsibility
ATO	air tasking order
C2	command and control
CAOC	combined air operations center
CCDR	combatant commander
COG	center of gravity
COMAFFOR	commander, Air Force forces
COMINT	communications intelligence
CSAF	Chief of Staff, US Air Force
CTO	cyber tasking order
DOD	Department of Defense
ELINT	electronic intelligence
EMS	electromagnetic spectrum
FISA	Foreign Intelligence Surveillance Act of 1978
GCC	global combatant commander
GIG	global information grid
HD	homeland defense
HUMINT	human intelligence
IMINT	imagery intelligence
IO	information operations
IP	Internet protocols
IPOE	intelligence preparation of the operational environment
ISR	intelligence, surveillance, and reconnaissance
JEFX	joint expeditionary force experiment
JFACC	joint force air component commander

JFC	joint force commander
JFCC	joint functional component command
JFCC-NW	Joint Functional Component Command – Network Warfare
JP	joint publication
JTF	joint task force
JTF-GNO	Joint Task Force – Global Network Operations
MAAP	master air attack plan
MAJCOM	major command
MOE	measures of effectiveness
MOP	measures of performance
NDS	national defense strategy
NMS	national military strategy
NMS-CO	National Military Strategy for Cyberspace Operations
OA	operational assessment
OODA	observe-orient-decide-act
OPCON	operational control
ROE	rules of engagement
ROMO	range of military operations
RF	radio frequency
SCADA	supervisory control and data acquisition
SECAF	Secretary, US Air Force
SIGINT	signals intelligence
SURF	single unit and retrieval format
TA	tactical assessment
TACON	tactical control
TTP	tactics, techniques and procedures
UAS	unmanned aircraft systems
UCP	unified command plan
US	United States
U.S.C.	United States Code
USSTRATCOM	United States Strategic Command
WMD	weapons of mass destruction

Definitions

administrative control. Direction or exercise of authority over subordinate or other organizations in respect to administration and support, including organization of Service forces, control of resources and equipment, personnel management, unit logistics, individual and unit training, readiness, mobilization, demobilization, discipline, and other matters not included in the operational missions of the subordinate or other organizations. Also called **ADCON**. (JP 1)

combatant command (command authority). Nontransferable command authority established by title 10 ("Armed Forces"), United States Code, section 164, exercised only by commanders of unified or specified combatant commands unless otherwise directed by the President or the Secretary of Defense. Combatant command (command authority) cannot be delegated and is the authority of a combatant commander to perform those functions of command over assigned forces involving organizing and employing commands and forces, assigning tasks, designating objectives, and giving authoritative direction over all aspects of military operations, joint training, and logistics necessary to accomplish the missions assigned to the command. Combatant command (authority) should be exercised through the commanders of subordinate organizations. Normally this authority is exercised through subordinate joint force commanders and Service and/or functional component commanders. Combatant command (command authority) provides full authority to organize and employ commands and forces as the combatant commander considers necessary to accomplish assigned missions. Operational control is inherent in combatant command (authority). Also called COCOM. (JP 1)

computer network exploitation. Enabling operations and intelligence collection capabilities conducted through the use of computer networks to gather data from target or adversary automated information systems or networks. Also called **CNE**. (JP 3-13)

cyber tasking order. Tasking document used by the AF cyber component commander to task assigned AF cyber forces to perform specific actions at specific time frames in support of AF and Joint requirements. Also called **CTO**. (AFDD 3-12)

cyberspace. Cyberspace is a global domain within the information environment consisting of the interdependent network of information technology infrastructures, including the Internet, telecommunications networks, computer systems, and embedded processors and controllers. (JP1-02) [*Cyberspace is a domain that requires man-made technology to enter and exploit. The only difference is that it is easier to see and sense the other domains. As with air and space, effects of cyberspace operations can occur simultaneously in many* *places. They can be precise, broad, enduring, and transitory.*] (AFDD 3-12) {Definition in brackets applies only to the Air Force and is offered for clarity.}

cyberspace defense. The passive, active and dynamic employment of capabilities to respond to imminent or on-going actions against AF or AF-protected networks, AF's portion of the Global Information Grid (GIG) or expeditionary communications assigned to the AF. (AFDD 3-12)

cyberspace force application. Combat operations in, through, and from cyberspace to achieve military objectives and influence the course and outcome of conflict by taking decisive actions against approved targets. (AFDD 3-12)

cyberspace operations. The employment of cyber capabilities where the primary purpose is to achieve objectives in or through cyberspace. (JP 3-0)

cyberspace superiority. The operational advantage in, through, and from cyberspace to conduct operations at a given time and in a given domain without prohibitive interference. (AFDD 3-12)

cyberspace support. Foundational, continuous or responsive operations in order to ensure information integrity and availability in, through, or from AF controlled infrastructure and its interconnected analog and digital portion of the battle space. (AFDD 3-12)

defensive counter cyberspace. A full range of active defensive measures taken to detect, identify, acquire information, track, and defend AF operations against actions or operations to penetrate, dissuade, degrade, disrupt, or corrupt friendly cyberspace freedom of action and capabilities. (AFDD 3-12)

design. A method of critical and creative thinking for understanding, visualizing, and describing complex, ill-structured problems and the approaches to resolve them. (AFDD 3-12)

electromagnetic spectrum. The range of frequencies of electromagnetic radiation from zero to infinity. It is divided into 26 alphabetically designated bands. Also called **EMS**. (JP 3-13.1)

electronic warfare. Military action involving the use of electromagnetic and directed energy to control the electromagnetic spectrum or to attack the enemy. Electronic warfare consists of three divisions: electronic attack, electronic protection, and electronic warfare support. Also called **EW**. (JP 3-13.1)

global information grid. The globally interconnected, end-to-end set of information capabilities, associated processes and personnel for collecting, processing, storing, disseminating, and managing information on demand to warfighters, policy makers, and support personnel. The global information grid includes owned and leased communications and computing systems and services, software (including applications), data, security services, other associated services and National Security Systems. Also called **GIG.** (JP 6-0)

global information infrastructure. The worldwide interconnection of communications networks, computers, databases, and consumer electronics that make vast amounts of information available to users. The global information infrastructure encompasses a wide range of equipment, including cameras, scanners, keyboards, facsimile machines, computers, switches, compact disks, video and audio tape, cable, wire, satellites, fiber optic transmission lines, networks of all types, televisions, monitors, printers, and much more. The friendly and adversary personnel who make decisions and handle the transmitted information constitute a critical component of the global information infrastructure. Also called **GII.** (JP 3-13)

global network operations center. United States Strategic Command operational element responsible for: providing global satellite communications system status; maintaining global situational awareness to include each combatant commander's planned and current operations as well as contingency plans; supporting radio frequency interference resolution management; supporting satellite anomaly resolution and management; facilitating satellite communications interface to the defense information infrastructure; and managing the regional satellite communications support centers. Also called **GNC.** (JP 6-0)

information assurance. Measures that protect and defend information and information systems by ensuring their availability, integrity, authentication, confidentiality, and non-repudiation. This includes providing for restoration of information systems by incorporating protection, detection, and reaction capabilities. (DODD 8500.01E, October 24, 2002 recertified April 23, 2007)

information environment. The aggregate of individuals, organizations, and systems that collect, process, disseminate, or act on information. (JP 3-13)

information operations. The integrated employment, during military operations, of information-related capabilities in concert with other lines of operation to influence, disrupt, corrupt, or usurp the decision-making of adversaries and potential adversaries while protecting our own. Also called **IO**. (SecDef Memo 12401-10)

joint force air component commander. The commander within a unified command, subordinate unified command, or joint task force responsible to the establishing commander for making recommendations on the proper employment of assigned, attached, and/or made available for tasking air forces; planning and coordinating air operations; or accomplishing such operational missions as may be assigned. Also called **JFACC**. See also **joint force commander**. (JP 3-0)

joint force commander. A general term applied to a combatant commander, subordinate unified commander, or joint task force commander authorized to exercise combatant command (command authority) or operational control over a joint force. Also called **JFC**. (JP 1)

malware. Software such as viruses or Trojans designed to cause damage or disruption to a computer system. (AFDD 3-12)

mission assurance (cyberspace). Measures required to accomplish essential objectives of missions in a contested environment. Mission assurance entails prioritizing mission essential functions, mapping mission dependence on cyberspace, identifying vulnerabilities, and mitigating risk of known vulnerabilities. (AFDD 3-12)

network defense. The employment of network-based capabilities to defend friendly information resident in or transiting through networks against adversary efforts to destroy, disrupt, corrupt, or usurp it. Also called **NetD**. (AFDD 3-13)

network operations. Activities to operate and defend the Global Information Grid. Also called **NetOps**. (JP 6-0)

offensive counter cyberspace. The operational planning and employment of capabilities to disrupt, deny, degrade, divert, neutralize or destroy an adversary's use of cyberspace capability or other data and information infrastructures to conduct activities or freedom of action. (AFDD 3-12)

operational control. Command authority that may be exercised by commanders at any echelon at or below the level of combatant command. Operational control is inherent in combatant command (command authority) and may be delegated within the command. Operational control is the authority to perform those functions of command over subordinate forces involving organizing and employing commands and forces, assigning tasks, designating objectives, and giving authoritative direction necessary to accomplish the mission. Operational control includes authoritative direction over all aspects of military operations and joint training necessary to accomplish missions assigned to the command. Operational control should be exercised through the commanders of subordinate organizations. Normally this authority is exercised through subordinate joint force commanders and Service and/or functional component commanders. Operational control normally provides full authority to organize commands and forces and to employ those forces as the commander in operational control considers necessary to accomplish assigned missions; it does not, in and of itself, include authoritative direction for logistics or matters of administration, discipline, internal organization, or unit training. Also called **OPCON**. (JP 1)

operations security. A process of identifying critical information and subsequently analyzing friendly actions attendant to military operations and other activities to: a. identify those actions that can be observed by adversary intelligence systems; b. determine indicators that adversary intelligence systems might obtain that could be interpreted or pieced together to derive critical information in time to be useful to adversaries; and c. select and execute measures that eliminate or reduce to an acceptable level the vulnerabilities of friendly actions to adversary exploitation. Also called **OPSEC**. (JP 3-13.3)

passive defense. Measures taken to reduce the probability of and to minimize the effects of damage caused by hostile action without the intention of taking the initiative. (JP 1-02) [*Continuous measures taken to secure and protect AF and DOD cyberspace assets through hardening and other measures against cyberspace attack and exploitation; identifying and mitigating vulnerabilities and employing capabilities to detect adversary activity and provide continual defense.*] (AFDD 3-12) {Definition in brackets applies only to the Air Force and is offered for clarity.}

tactical control. Command authority over assigned or attached forces or commands, or military capability or forces made available for tasking, that is limited to the detailed direction and control of movements or maneuvers within the operational area necessary to accomplish missions or tasks assigned. Tactical control is inherent in operational control. Tactical control may be delegated to, and exercised at any level at or below the level of combatant command. Tactical control provides sufficient authority for controlling and directing the application of force or tactical use of combat support assets within the assigned mission or task. Also called **TACON**. (JP 1)

www.ingramcontent.com/pod-product-compliance
Lightning Source LLC
Chambersburg PA
CBHW080542290526
45790CB00006B/2520